I0814288

COLLEGE SPORTS ENCYCLOPEDIAS

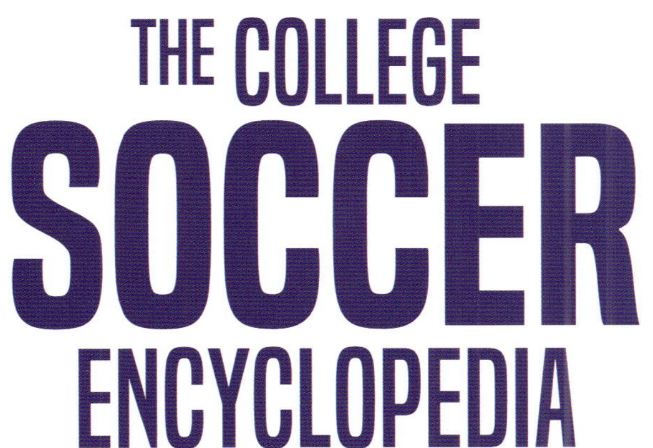

THE COLLEGE SOCCER ENCYCLOPEDIA

BY CHARLIE BEATTIE

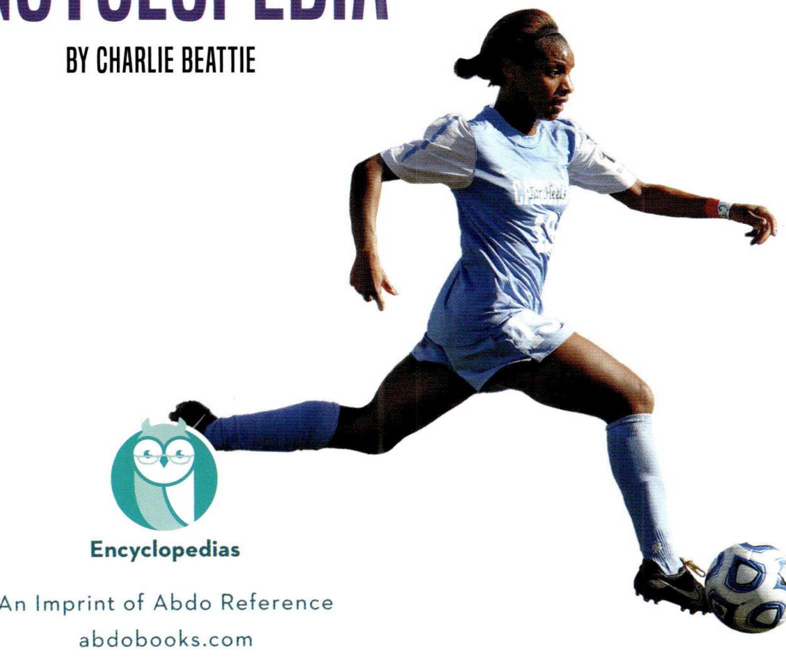

Encyclopedias

An Imprint of Abdo Reference

abdobooks.com

TABLE OF CONTENTS

VERMONT
28

THE HISTORY OF COLLEGE SOCCER

Soccer is a global sport. Whether on city streets, at local parks, or in massive stadiums, people play the game all over the world. In the United States, the soccer landscape includes a thriving college scene. Though sometimes overshadowed by the professional game, college soccer has a long and rich history.

What is recognized as the first college soccer game took place on November 6, 1869. Rutgers beat Princeton, then known as the College of New Jersey, 6–4. This game might sound familiar to fans of college football. That's because it's also known as the birth of that sport. However, the game actually had more similarities to modern soccer than football. For example, carrying the ball was illegal,

Nick Scardina, *left*, of Washington defends Clemson's Hamady Diop in the 2021 men's College Cup final.

THE SOCCER BOWL

In 1950, four men's teams met in St. Louis for the first postseason college soccer tournament. It was called the Soccer Bowl. Penn State and San Francisco tied 2–2 in the final. There was no extra time in that era, so both teams were declared champions. However, Soccer Bowl champions were not necessarily recognized by the ISFA. In 1951, Penn State won the tournament, but the ISFA recognized West Chester as the national champion. The last Soccer Bowl was played in 1952.

and players scored by kicking the ball into a goal. Each goal was worth one point.

The modern rules of soccer were established in the late 1800s in Great Britain. Around this time, the game began spreading to countries all over the world. However, while the sport took off elsewhere, it grew more slowly in the United States. This was in part due to the booming popularity of other American sports, such as baseball and football. As a result, in the early 1900s, few American colleges had soccer teams. Those that did were so spread out that scheduling games was difficult.

For the first half of the century, fewer than 50 schools participated in soccer, and the players were almost exclusively men. The Intercollegiate Soccer Football Association (ISFA) oversaw the sport. There was no national championship tournament. Instead, starting in 1904, the ISFA began recognizing champions based on regular-season performance. Haverford College of Pennsylvania was the first champion.

POSTWAR GROWTH

International soccer began to grow in popularity during the 1920s. That led to the creation of the men's World Cup in 1930. The sport really began to take off after World War II (1939–45), including at the college level. Many American military members had been stationed in foreign countries where the sport was more popular. Soccer became a popular sport for the US soldiers as they tried to stay in shape. When those soldiers returned home, many of them went to college. There, they formed teams at their new schools.

By the end of the 1950s, there were roughly 250 college teams spread around the country. The National Collegiate Athletic Association (NCAA) took notice and decided to put on

Members of the Lincoln University soccer team pose for a photo after a game in 1949.

an official men's championship tournament. The first edition took place in 1959. Eight teams gathered in Storrs, Connecticut, to play single-elimination games. In the final, Saint Louis defeated Bridgeport 5–2 to become the first NCAA champion. The tournament is still held today, but now 48 teams take part each year. The last two rounds are known as the College Cup.

Saint Louis dominated the tournament in its early years. Soccer had been popular in the city for decades. The Billikens drew from mostly local talent to build the sport's first powerhouse. By 1973, Saint Louis had won or shared ten national titles.

The Billikens' opponents at the first College Cup represented just how diverse NCAA soccer schools were at the time. While Saint Louis has long had a major athletic department, other early soccer powers came from much smaller programs. In addition to Bridgeport, the other semifinalists in 1959 were West Chester and City College of New York. Throughout the 1960s and 1970s, a mix of small and large schools continued

HISTORIC HOWARD

Howard University, a historically Black school located in Washington, DC, built a powerful men's soccer program in the early 1970s. The Bison went undefeated in 1971 and beat Saint Louis 3–2 to win the College Cup. That title was later vacated by the NCAA, which ruled Howard had used ineligible players. The Bison won again in 1974. Howard's championship was the first Division I title won in any sport by a team from a historically Black college.

The NCAA separated into three divisions in 1973. But many small schools still chose to play Division I soccer.

to make up the top level of college men's soccer. Even after the NCAA introduced multiple divisions in the early 1970s, many small schools still played soccer in Division I, the highest level in the NCAA. Tiny Hartwick College won the tournament as late as 1977. Hartwick stayed in Division I in men's soccer until 2018, when the New York school dropped to Division III.

WOMEN'S SOCCER ARRIVES

In 1972, the United States passed Title IX. The law stated that any institution receiving federal money could not discriminate

The North Carolina Tar Heels have been the dominant program in women's college soccer for over 40 years.

based on gender. Though Title IX was not intended as a sports bill, it ended up having a massive impact on sports. That's because public high schools and colleges typically had many more sports teams for men than they did for women. Title IX required these schools to provide equal opportunities, which meant they had to create more women's sports teams. As a result, women's college soccer grew throughout the 1970s and 1980s.

At the time, the NCAA sanctioned only men's sports. An organization called the Association for Intercollegiate Athletics for Women (AIAW) formed in 1971 to govern college women's sports. Yet even the AIAW didn't sanction a women's soccer tournament until 1981. That was the only AIAW soccer championship, however, as the NCAA began sponsoring women's soccer the next year. The women's tournament now includes 64 teams. The final two rounds are nicknamed the College Cup in both the women's and men's tournaments.

Coach Anson Dorrance's North Carolina Tar Heels beat Central Florida 1–0 for the 1981 AIAW title. The two teams met again the following year in the first NCAA title game. This time, North Carolina won 2–0. The Tar Heels went on to appear in every College Cup final through the 1994 season. In that time, the Tar Heels lost the championship game only once.

PROFESSIONAL OPPORTUNITIES

For many years, opportunities to play professional soccer in the United States were limited. On the men's side, the North American Soccer League was founded in 1968. The league enjoyed some spurts of great popularity before folding in 1984. The US Men's National Team (USMNT) struggled for success and popularity during this time. After competing in the 1950 World Cup, the Americans went 40 years without qualifying again.

All the while, men's college soccer carried on. New dynasties followed Saint Louis. Indiana won three NCAA championships during the 1980s. In the early 1990s, Virginia became the first men's team to win four straight titles.

When the USMNT finally returned to the World Cup in 1990, its roster was filled with college players. Paul Caligiuri scored the goal that secured the team's qualification. He was one of four former University of California, Los Angeles (UCLA) players on the team. Many former college stars also represented the United States at the 1994 World Cup on home soil. The success of that tournament led to the formation of Major League Soccer (MLS) two years later, in 1996.

Women's soccer also experienced great growth in the 1980s and 1990s. The US Women's National Team (USWNT) played its first games in 1985. By 1991, the USWNT was an international power and won the first Women's World Cup. Current or former college athletes played a big role in the team's early success. Star players including North Carolina's April Heinrichs and Central Florida's Michelle Akers honed their skills playing college soccer.

The 1999 Women's World Cup was held in the United States. Among the USWNT's 20 players, eight had ties to North Carolina, including the team's star forward, Mia Hamm. That team captured the nation's attention on the way to a second world championship.

Attempts to develop a women's professional league proved difficult. Two early attempts failed. Organizers finally got it right with the creation of

After starring at Saint Louis, midfielder Matt McKeon was the first player taken in MLS's first college draft in 1996.

the National Women's Soccer League (NWSL) in 2012. It is now one of the world's premier women's soccer leagues.

MLS and the NWSL continue to provide professional opportunities for many former college soccer players. There are also minor leagues. In addition, more American players are joining professional teams overseas.

The growth of professional and international soccer has helped spur growth in college soccer as well. The number of college men's teams at all levels grew by roughly 200 from 1980 to 2000, for a total of 719. The expansion of women's soccer was even greater. In 1982, there were only 77 women's teams. By 2000, there were 790.

Michelle Akers joined the USWNT in 1985, just after her freshman season at Central Florida.

NEW DYNASTIES

Even as more schools created women's soccer teams, North Carolina remained dominant. Between 2000 and 2009, the Tar Heels added five more titles. The men's game was much more wide-open. While traditional powers such as Indiana,

Virginia, and UCLA all won championships in the decade, new champions such as the University of California, Santa Barbara (UC Santa Barbara) and Akron also emerged.

The rest of the country finally caught up to the North Carolina women's team in the 2010s. During the decade, no team repeated as champion in women's soccer. Meanwhile, the men's game witnessed its longest-running dynasty since Virginia in the early 1990s. Entering the 2015 season, Stanford had never won a national title. That year, the Cardinal won the first of three straight.

By 2020, college soccer teams were stocked with talent from both the United States and overseas. Of the 32 teams that competed in the 2023 Women's World Cup, 21 featured at least one player who played NCAA soccer.

ADAPTING THE GAME

For many years, the NCAA served as the main pipeline for developing US professional soccer players. That eventually began to change, especially in the 2000s. As the sport became more popular at all levels, more opportunities arose for top youth players. For example, every MLS team now operates a

Stanford's women's team holds up the trophy after winning the 2017 NCAA title. It was one of three championships the Cardinal won in the 2010s.

youth academy. Professional teams in Europe have a similar model for developing young players.

College soccer allows players to get an education while playing the game at a competitive level. However, critics noted that the NCAA's shorter seasons and nontraditional rules didn't align well with professional soccer. As a result, many

THE MAC HERMANN TROPHY

The annual Hermann Trophy was first awarded to the top player in men's college soccer in 1967. A women's winner was added in 1988. Over the years, the Missouri Athletic Club (MAC) and United Soccer Coaches created their own competing awards. By 2002, the three organizations had unified around a single player of the year award. Today, the MAC Hermann Trophy is awarded to the top man and top woman in college soccer each season.

observers viewed these academies as a better option than college teams for young players hoping to play professionally.

One way college soccer differs from international soccer is the game clock. Typically, soccer uses a running clock with stoppage time added

Players from North Carolina and Charlotte battle in a 2011 men's College Cup game.

to the end of each half. But in college soccer, the clock counts down and pauses during stoppages in play. These changes can affect the gameplay, especially at the end of a half.

College soccer also uses different rules for substitutions. In international soccer, a team can make five substitutions per game. A player who is taken out of the game cannot return.

Virginia's Daryl Dike celebrates a goal in the 2019 NCAA men's title game. He went on to play professionally and for the USMNT.

Tar Heels
19

Alessia Russo (19) starred at North Carolina in the late 2010s. Russo scored three goals for England at the 2023 Women's World Cup.

But college soccer allows unlimited substitutions. Also, for many years a player taken out in the first half could come back in during the second half.

The NCAA has begun adapting some of its rules to better align with international soccer. Since 2024, college teams can make substitutions only at six specific points in a game, and players taken out cannot reenter. This is closer to international rules.

The NCAA was also considering making the season longer. Instead of just playing in the fall, players would now practice, train, and play throughout the school year. That schedule would better match the professional leagues around the world.

MEN'S TEAMS
AKRON ZIPS

Darlington Nagbe (6) won the MAC Hermann Trophy in 2010. He was the second Zips player to win the award in as many years.

Akron's men's soccer team was founded in 1955. In their first year, the Zips finished 2–4–1. Over the next 70 years, the program suffered only three more losing seasons.

The Zips dominated the Ohio College Soccer Association. They appeared in their first NCAA Tournament in 1961. But winning in the tournament was tougher. Akron didn't advance past the second round until 1986. That year, the Zips reached the final against heavily favored Duke. The Blue Devils won 1–0.

One of Duke's players from that game, Ken Lolla, became Akron's coach in 1993. In his final season in 2005, Lolla led the Zips to the Elite Eight. It was the team's deepest NCAA Tournament run in two decades.

The Zips' most successful era came in the following years under new coach Caleb Porter. He built a strong defensive structure. In 2009, Akron set a national record by allowing only seven goals in 25 games. The No. 1–ranked Zips didn't allow a single goal in five NCAA Tournament games. However, they were upset in the final by No. 2 Virginia. After a scoreless draw, the Cavaliers won on penalty kicks.

Akron goalkeeper David Meves set an NCAA record with 55 shutouts between 2009 and 2012.

Akron players celebrate after beating Louisville 1–0 to win the 2010 NCAA title.

BARSON SAVES THE DAY

Chad Barson didn't score in Akron's 2010 national title win over Louisville. But the defender made two huge plays. In the first half, Barson made a save on the goal line with goalkeeper David Meves out of position. In the final minute, Meves made a big save, but the rebound deflected to Louisville's Aaron Horton. Horton took a shot from straight on, but Barson scrambled back to knock it away.

Akron suffered only one regular-season loss the next season. The Zips survived a shootout against California in the Elite Eight to reach the 2010 College Cup. The Zips then beat Michigan 2–1 in the semifinals to set up a title game against Louisville, which was then coached by Lolla.

With just over 11 minutes to play, the game was still scoreless. Akron midfielder Scott Caldwell's shot was blocked in the penalty area. The ball bounced straight back to the sophomore. This time he hammered home the championship-winning goal.

Porter left after the 2012 season to begin a long career coaching in the professional ranks. Several Akron players from this era also went on to pro careers, including forward Teal Bunbury and midfielder Darlington Nagbe. They were the MAC Hermann Trophy winners in 2009 and 2010, respectively. Akron has remained competitive in the years since, with the 2018 team again finishing as the NCAA runner-up.

FACT BOX

First Season: 1955

Location: Akron, Ohio

Stadium: FirstEnergy Stadium

Conference: Big East Conference

All-Time Record: 791–302–120

NCAA Tournament Appearances: 36

College Cup Appearances: 6

National Titles: 2010

Top Coaches: Ken Lolla (1993–2005); Caleb Porter (2006–12); Jared Embick (2013–)

Top Players: Pete Milich (1960–63); George Nanchoff (1973–76); Derek Gaffney (1983–86); Steve Zakuani (2007–08); Teal Bunbury (2008–09); Darlington Nagbe (2008–10); David Meves (2009–12); Scott Caldwell (2009–12)

Mascot: Zippy

CLEMSON TIGERS

Clemson's Jody DeBruin brings the ball up the field during a 1997 game.

Clemson began its men's soccer program in 1934. But the team lasted only six years before it was disbanded. Chemistry professor I. M. Ibrahim revived the team in 1967. By 1972, the Tigers were a powerhouse in the Atlantic Coast Conference (ACC). That year, Clemson won the first of eight straight ACC titles. The Tigers also appeared in the NCAA Tournament for the first time.

Clemson was even better in the 1980s. Ibrahim coached the Tigers to a national championship in 1984 and again in 1987. Clemson won its second title at its home stadium of Riggs Field, the host site for that year's College Cup.

Ibrahim left the team in 1994. Though the Tigers remained a contender, they reached the College Cup only once in the next two decades. When Mike Noonan took over as coach in 2010, the program was coming off three straight losing seasons.

Clemson fans cheer on the Tigers at the 2021 College Cup.

The Tigers went three more years without a winning record before returning to the NCAA Tournament in 2013. By 2015, Noonan had guided them back to the College Cup final.

Ousmane Sylla waves to the crowd after scoring in the 2023 College Cup final against Notre Dame.

Clemson lost 4–0 to Stanford in that year's championship. But the Tigers were primed for more success. Clemson won the 2021 College Cup 2–0 over Washington. Forward Isaiah Reid scored the first goal just 25 seconds into the game. He added a second 14 minutes later on a header.

Two years later, the Tigers reached the 2023 championship game against Notre Dame. Midfielder Brandon Parrish scored from long range in the first half. Star forward Ousmane

PALMETTO PRIDE

Games in all sports between Clemson and South Carolina are known as the Palmetto Series. The men's soccer game between the two schools is traditionally the first game of the Palmetto Series. In 2023, Clemson won the rivalry game for the 34th time.

Sylla tapped in the eventual winning goal with just over 20 minutes to go. Clemson held on for a 2–1 win.

The victory capped a big year for Sylla. He became the fourth Tiger to win the MAC Hermann Trophy. He joined school legends Bruce Murray (1987), Wojtek Krakowiak (1998), and Robbie Robinson (2019).

FACT BOX

First Season: 1934

Location: Clemson, South Carolina

Stadium: Riggs Field

Conference: Atlantic Coast Conference

All-Time Record: 759–296–107

NCAA Tournament Appearances: 36

College Cup Appearances: 10

National Titles: 1984, 1987, 2021, 2023

Top Coaches: I. M. Ibrahim (1967–94); Trevor Adair (1995–2008); Mike Noonan (2010–)

Top Players: Nnamdi Nwokocha (1979–82); Gary Conner (1983–86); Bruce Murray (1984–87); Jimmy Glenn (1990–93); Wolde Harris (1993–95); Wojtek Krakowiak (1997–98); Robbie Robinson (2017–19); Ousmane Sylla (2020–23)

Mascot: The Tiger

CONNECTICUT HUSKIES

UConn's John Blomstrann, *center*, tries to stop a Brown University player during a 1975 game.

Connecticut founded its men's soccer program in 1928. After a slow start, the team disbanded for three seasons during World War II (1939–45). When coach John Squires re-formed the Huskies in 1946, the team took off.

Squires coached the team better known as UConn through 1968. His replacement would soon become the most famous name in program history. Joseph J. Morrone tirelessly raised funds for the team, eventually securing more than $2 million to turn the men's soccer team into an elite program. Much of that money went to a new stadium, which is now named after the Hall of Fame coach.

One of Morrone's top players was his son, Joseph M. Morrone. Known as Joe Jr., the younger Morrone graduated in 1980 as the program's all-time leading scorer. In his senior year, he also became UConn's first MAC Hermann Trophy winner.

Coach Joseph J. Morrone won 358 games at UConn from 1969 to 1996.

Despite losing Joe Jr., the Huskies remained a strong team in 1981. They reached the College Cup for the first time. UConn then defeated

UConn's Chris Gbandi goes airborne to kick the ball during the 2000 NCAA championship game against Creighton.

Eastern Illinois 2–1 before beating Alabama A&M by the same score in extra time to win the team's first championship.

UConn reached the College Cup twice more under Morrone, who coached until 1996. New coach Ray Reid took the Huskies back to the championship game in 2000. MAC Hermann Trophy winner Chris Gbandi and forward Darin Lewis scored in a 2–0 win over Creighton.

Despite years of success, the program slipped in the late 2010s. In 2022, Gbandi took over for Reid and became just the program's third head coach since 1968. Gbandi led UConn back to winning records in both 2023 and 2024.

THE FIRST CHAMPIONS

UConn claims three national championships in men's soccer. The first came in 1948. Led by coach John Squires, that year's team finished a perfect 11–0. College soccer had no national tournament at the time. The Huskies were crowned champions in a vote by the National Soccer Coaches Association of America.

FACT BOX

First Season: 1928

Location: Storrs, Connecticut

Stadium: Morrone Stadium

Conference: Big East Conference

All-Time Record: 859–525–145

NCAA Tournament Appearances: 36

College Cup Appearances: 5

National Titles: 1981, 2000

Top Coaches: John Squires (1937–42, 1946–68); Joseph J. Morrone (1969–96); Ray Reid (1997–21)

Top Players: Joseph M. Morrone (1977–80); Elvis Comrie (1978–81); Pedro DeBrito (1978–81); Daniel Donigan (1985–88); Chris Gbandi (1998–2001); O'Brian White (2005–08); Josh Ford (2007–10); Andre Blake (2011–13)

Mascot: Jonathan the Husky

CREIGHTON BLUEJAYS

Bob Warming coached Creighton from 1990 to 1994 and from 2001 to 2009.

Creighton first fielded a men's soccer team in 1979. The Bluejays posted a 34–18–5 record over their first three years. But after following that with three losing seasons, the school abandoned the soccer program in 1986.

Creighton retook the field in 1990. The Bluejays quickly became a strong team again. Under the leadership of coach Bob Warming and then Bret Simon, Creighton reached the NCAA Tournament each season from 1992 to 2008.

The Bluejays reached the College Cup for the first time in 1996 before losing in the semifinals. Four years later, Simon guided Creighton to its greatest season yet. The Bluejays led the nation with a school-record 22 wins in 2010. In the College Cup semifinals, they beat Indiana in triple extra time. However, Creighton fell to UConn 2–0 in the final.

Simon left the program after the 2000 season. Warming returned and kept Creighton's streak of qualifying for the NCAA Tournament going. In 2002, the team got back to the College Cup. The Bluejays also moved into Morrison Stadium in 2003. There, they have consistently ranked among the top NCAA teams in attendance. Warming left for good in 2009.

Under new coach Elmar Bolowich, the Bluejays once again reached the College Cup in 2012. They also moved into the highly competitive Big East Conference in 2013. Despite the change in conference, the team remained among the contenders. Creighton also continued to produce top players.

Creighton players celebrate the team's game-winning goal in extra time during the 2000 College Cup semifinals against Indiana.

Creighton midfielder Giorgio Probo controls the ball against Syracuse in the 2022 College Cup semifinals.

THE DODGE STREET DERBY

Creighton shares a city with the University of Nebraska Omaha. The two schools met seven times from 1979 to 1982. The rivalry was renewed in 2016, and the schools now play every season. The rivalry is nicknamed "The Dodge Street Derby" after one of Omaha's major roads. Creighton picked up its eighth win in the series in 2024.

Bolowich coached seven first-team All-Americans in his eight seasons in charge.

In 2022, junior forward Duncan McGuire scored an NCAA-best 23 goals and became the school's second MAC Hermann Trophy winner. The first was Johnny Torres in 1997. When McGuire won the award, Torres was his coach. He had taken over for Bolowich in 2019, hoping to lead his alma mater to its first national championship.

FACT BOX

First Season: 1979

Location: Omaha, Nebraska

Stadium: Morrison Stadium

Conference: Big East Conference

All-Time Record: 521–227–90

NCAA Tournament Appearances: 26

College Cup Appearances: 6

National Titles: None

Top Coaches: Bob Warming (1990–94, 2001–09); Bret Simon (1995–2000); Elmar Bolowich (2011–18)

Top Players: Keith DeFini (1990–93); Johnny Torres (1994–97); Richard Mulrooney (1995–98); Mike Tranchilla (1999–2002); Brian Holt (2008–11); Ethan Finlay (2008–11); Fabian Herbers (2013–15); Duncan McGuire (2020–22)

Mascot: Billy Bluejay

DUKE BLUE DEVILS

Duke had fielded a successful men's soccer team for decades before participating in its first NCAA Tournament in 1972. The Blue Devils lost their opening game 9–0 to Howard. Within a decade, however, Duke was a national power.

Coach John Rennie's team was No. 1 in the country entering the 1982 NCAA Tournament. Duke reached the final against Indiana. The Hoosiers won 2–1 in a marathon game that took eight extra time periods.

Many of Rennie's freshmen from that team were seniors in 1986. The coach built his team to play strong defense. Duke allowed only four goals in four NCAA Tournament games leading up to the championship against underdog Akron.

Early in the second half, Duke forward Tom Stone collected a loose ball off a deflected free kick. Standing just outside the six-yard box, Stone volleyed in the only goal of

Duke's Jeremy Ebobisse controls the ball during a game in 2015.

John Kerr captained Duke's 1986 championship team and later became the Blue Devils' coach.

the game. It was Stone's 16th goal of the season, eight of which were game-winning strikes.

Rennie coached the Blue Devils through the 2007 season. He won 410 games. The legendary coach also led Duke to three more College Cups. Duke lost to rival Virginia in the 1992 semifinals. After beating the Cavaliers in 1995, Duke fell 2–0 to Wisconsin in the championship game. The Blue Devils fell in the semifinals again in 2004, this time to UC Santa Barbara.

A CAMPUS FIRST

Duke's 1986 championship was the first team sports title in the school's history in any sport. The win kicked off a successful 25-year run. By 2019, Duke had won 17 team national championships, split among men's basketball, men's lacrosse, women's tennis, and women's golf.

Duke's Brian White celebrates a goal against Fordham in the 2017 NCAA Tournament.

One of Rennie's former star players, John Kerr, took over as coach in 2008. Kerr had scored 42 goals during his Duke playing career and was a star on the Blue Devils' 1986 championship team. That year, he also won the MAC Hermann Trophy. Kerr was the fourth Duke player in five seasons to win the prestigious honor. Joe Ulrich (1982), Mike Jeffries (1983), and Tom Kain (1985) were the others.

Ali Curtis became the fifth Blue Devil to win it in 1999. The star forward tied the program record with 17 goals that season. Andrew Wenger matched that record and won the Hermann Trophy in 2011. Through 2025, only Indiana had more than Duke's six winners.

FACT BOX

First Season: 1935

Location: Durham, North Carolina

Stadium: Koskinen Stadium

Conference: Atlantic Coast Conference

All-Time Record: 782–430–105

NCAA Tournament Appearances: 30

College Cup Appearances: 5

National Titles: 1986

Top Coaches: John Rennie (1979–2007); John Kerr (2008–)

Top Players: Joe Ulrich (1981–82); Mike Jeffries (1980–83); Tom Kain (1982–85); John Kerr (1983–86); Jason Kreis (1991–94); Ali Curtis (1997–2000); Andrew Wenger (2009–11)

Mascot: The Blue Devil

GEORGETOWN HOYAS

Georgetown forward Brandon Allen splits Saint John's defenders during the 2012 Big East Tournament.

One year after disbanding its football team, Georgetown created a men's soccer team in 1952. The new team attracted some interest from the school's many international students. However, for their first several seasons, the Hoyas weren't very competitive. A big reason for the team's struggles was its lack of scholarships. It didn't begin offering a full slate of scholarships until 2005.

Georgetown did find some success in the years prior. Keith Tabatznik took over as coach in 1984, and he led the team for 22 seasons. In 1994, the Hoyas reached their first NCAA Tournament. The Hoyas also won their first Big East Conference title that year. Meanwhile, Ben McKnight's 18 goals and 46 points remained team records two decades later.

Tabatznik led the team through 2005, leaving with a career record of 220–187–23. Brian Wiese replaced him the following year. With more scholarships, Wiese was able to attract higher-skilled players. In 2012, the Hoyas got on a roll and made it all the way to the NCAA championship game. Though they fell 1–0 to powerhouse Indiana, the Hoyas showed they could compete among the sport's best.

Under Wiese, Georgetown has remained strong. In 2019, the Hoyas returned to the NCAA final. This time they outlasted Virginia in a shootout to claim the program's first national title.

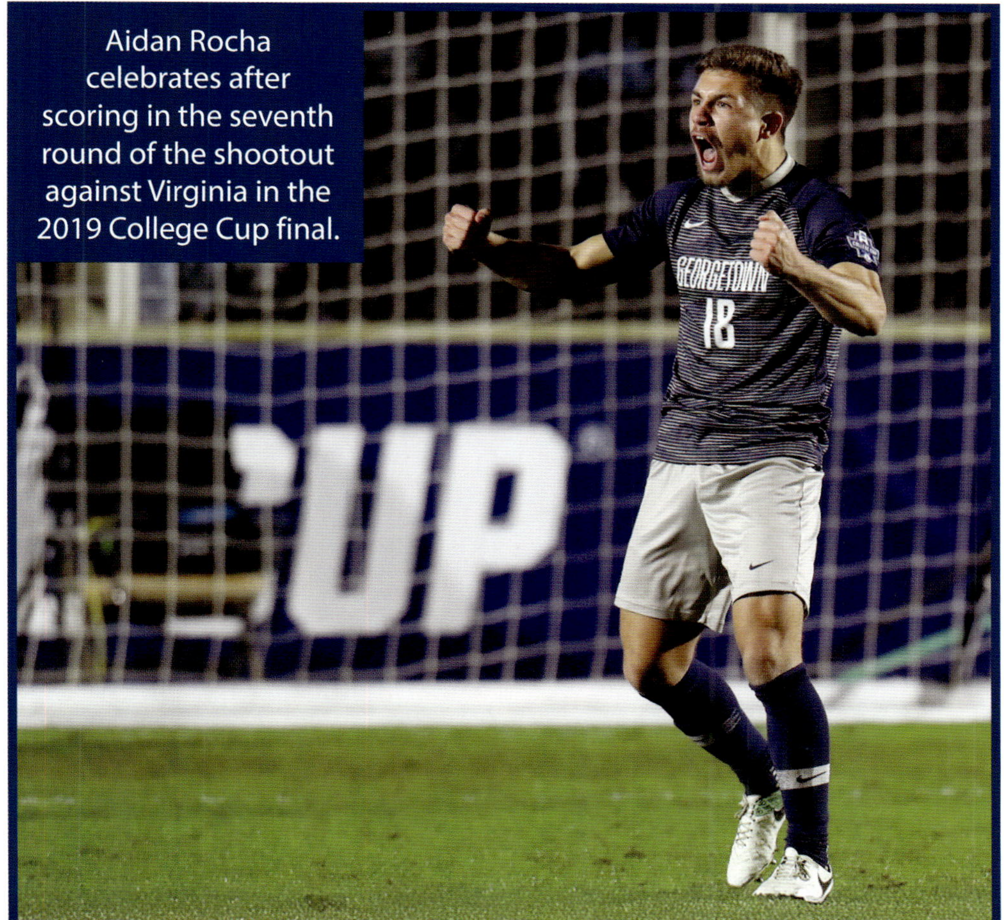

Aidan Rocha celebrates after scoring in the seventh round of the shootout against Virginia in the 2019 College Cup final.

UNEXPECTED OFFENSE

The 2019 NCAA final featured the sport's two best defenses. Surprisingly, the game turned into an offensive showcase. Georgetown and Virginia played to a 3–3 tie. It was the highest-scoring title game since 1980. Finally, after seven rounds in a shootout, the Hoyas prevailed. Goalkeeper Tomas Romero made the decisive diving save to clinch the national title.

Hoyas midfielder Joe DaLuz, *right*, battles with a Washington player for the ball during the 2021 College Cup semifinals.

The Hoyas nearly got back to the title game two years later. However, they fell to Washington in the semifinals.

A run of great Georgetown players arrived in the 2010s. Goalkeeper Tomas Gomez recorded a team-record 36 shutouts between 2011 and 2014. Forward Brandon Allen left the team in 2015 after setting a new standard with 50 goals. That same year, Allen became the first Georgetown player to be named a finalist for the MAC Hermann Trophy. Defender Dylan Nealis also became a finalist in 2019. And in 2021, midfielder Dante Polvara became Georgetown's first Hermann Trophy winner after recording seven goals and six assists in 22 games.

FACT BOX

First Season: 1952

Location: Washington, DC

Stadium: Shaw Field

Conference: Big East Conference

All-Time Record: 559–502–103

NCAA Tournament Appearances: 15

College Cup Appearances: 3

National Titles: 2019

Top Coaches: Keith Tabatznik (1984–2005); Brian Wiese (2006–)

Top Players: Ben McKnight (1992–95); Tomas Gomez (2011–14); Brandon Allen (2012–15); Joshua Yaro (2013–15); Dylan Nealis (2016–19); Giannis Nikopolidis (2018–21); Sean Zawadzki (2018–21); Dante Polvara (2019–21)

Mascot: Jack the Bulldog

INDIANA HOOSIERS

Indiana coach Jerry Yeagley, *center*, celebrates with his team after winning the 2003 NCAA title. Yeagley's 543 wins are the most by any Division I coach at one school.

Indiana first fielded a men's varsity soccer team in 1973. The Hoosiers finished the first season 12–2, outscoring their opponents 68–7. That marked the beginning of one of the sport's most successful programs.

Under coach Jerry Yeagley, Indiana reached its first College Cup just three years later, in 1976. The Hoosiers lost the final to San Francisco. Indiana also came up short in its next two College Cup visits. But the team broke through in dramatic fashion in 1982. Indiana and Duke played into eight extra time periods in the final. After 159 minutes and 16 seconds of play, Indiana's Gregg Thompson curled in a free kick to give the Hoosiers a 2–1 win. At the time, it was the longest game in college soccer history.

The win kicked off a new era of success under Yeagley, who coached the Hoosiers until 2003. From September 1983 to November 1984, Indiana played an NCAA-record 46 straight games without losing. That stretch included the Hoosiers' second straight national championship.

Indiana goalkeeper Jay Nolly makes a save in the shootout against UC Santa Barbara in the 2004 College Cup final.

Yeagley's teams added NCAA titles in 1988, 1998, 1999, and 2003, just before he retired. Yeagley coached 27 All-Americans. Five Hoosiers won the MAC Hermann Trophy during Yeagley's tenure. Forward Ken Snow, the school's all-time leading scorer, won the award twice, in 1988 and 1990.

After Yeagley retired, assistant Mike Freitag took over in 2004. That season, he led the program to the national title

ONE LOSING SEASON

Indiana finally experienced a losing season in 2013, 40 years after the program was founded. The Hoosiers finished the regular season 6–11–1. But Indiana found its rhythm in the Big Ten Tournament. The Hoosiers defeated Michigan State 1–0 in the final. Because of that result, Indiana still qualified for the NCAA Tournament.

Harrison Petts (7) holds up the championship trophy after Indiana's 1–0 victory over Georgetown in the 2012 College Cup final.

with a shootout win over UC Santa Barbara. It marked the third time Indiana had won back-to-back titles.

Freitag left after the 2009 season, and a new member of the Yeagley family took over. Jerry's son Todd Yeagley had been a four-time All-American while playing for the Hoosiers from 1991 to 1994. In 2012, he led Indiana to its eighth national title. Only Saint Louis, with ten, had more.

On November 24, 2024, Yeagley led Indiana to a 2–1 extra time victory over Akron in the first round of the NCAA Tournament. It was the Hoosiers' 105th NCAA Tournament win since 1973. No Division I school had more.

FACT BOX

First Season: 1973

Location: Bloomington, Indiana

Stadium: Bill Armstrong Stadium

Conference: Big Ten Conference

All-Time Record: 833–203–122

NCAA Tournament Appearances: 49

College Cup Appearances: 22

National Titles: 1982, 1983, 1988, 1998, 1999, 2003, 2004, 2012

Top Coaches: Jerry Yeagley (1973–2003); Mike Freitag (2004–09); Todd Yeagley (2010–)

Top Players: Angelo DiBernardo (1976–78); Armando Betancourt (1979–81); Ken Snow (1987–90); Brian Maisonneuve (1991–94); Todd Yeagley (1991–94); Danny O'Rourke (2001–04); Andrew Gutman (2015–18); Roman Celentano (2019–21)

Mascot: None

MARSHALL THUNDERING HERD

Marshall began its soccer program in 1979. Forty years later, the team had not accomplished much. The Thundering Herd had mostly endured losing seasons. Marshall's only conference title had come in 2000, when the team was a member of the Midwest Athletic Conference (MAC).

In 2016, the Thundering Herd won just six games and failed to qualify for the Conference USA tournament. After the season, longtime coach Bob Gray retired. Chris Grassie replaced him.

The new coach quickly brought improvement. In 2019, Marshall won 16 games and reached the

Marshall coach Chris Grassie, *center*, huddles with his team before the 2024 College Cup final.

NCAA Tournament for the first time. The Thundering Herd also won their first tournament game. They beat in-state rival West Virginia 2–1 before falling to Washington in the next round.

Marshall returned to the tournament the next season. Due to the COVID-19 pandemic, that season was delayed until the spring of 2021.

ROBERTS TO THE RESCUE

Marshall's Jamil Roberts had a 2020 NCAA Tournament to remember. After scoring just two goals all season, Roberts scored the game-winner against Georgetown to put Marshall into the College Cup. He then added game-winning goals against North Carolina in the semifinal and Indiana in the championship game.

Vitor Dias had 14 goals and 15 assists in three seasons at Marshall from 2019 to 2021.

Marshall finished the shortened regular season 9–2–2. It then made a run through a tough NCAA Tournament schedule. After beating Fordham in the first round, the Thundering Herd knocked off No. 1–ranked Clemson in a shootout. Marshall then beat defending national champion Georgetown 1–0 to reach its first College Cup.

Jamil Roberts celebrates after Marshall's victory over Indiana in the College Cup final held in spring 2021.

After beating North Carolina in the semifinals, the upstart Thundering Herd faced traditional power Indiana in the final. The game was scoreless in extra time when Marshall midfielder Vitor Dias maneuvered into the Hoosiers' penalty area. Dias's first shot was blocked straight back to him. His second attempt was saved by the Indiana goalkeeper but deflected off the crossbar and then off the far post. The ball finally settled in front of Marshall forward Jamil Roberts, who scored from close range to win the game and the championship.

FACT BOX

First Season: 1979

Location: Huntington, West Virginia

Stadium: Veterans Memorial Soccer Complex

Conference: Sun Belt Conference

All-Time Record: 393–401–80

NCAA Tournament Appearances: 6

College Cup Appearances: 2

National Titles: 2020

Top Coaches: Bob Gray (1995–2016); Chris Grassie (2017–)

Top Players: Andy Zulauf (1981–85); Mark Taylor (1987–90); Byron Carmichael (1999–2002); Brad Puryear (1982–85); Taly Goode (1996–2000); Pedro Dolabella (2017–21); Vitor Dias (2019–21); Matthew Bell (2022–23)

Mascot: Marco the Bison

Marshall switched conferences again in 2023, moving to the Sun Belt. But the team continued its successful run under Grassie. In 2024, Marshall played in its sixth straight NCAA Tournament. The Thundering Herd advanced to the title game once again. This time they fell 2–1 in extra time to Vermont.

MARYLAND TERRAPINS

Maryland plays its home games at Ludwig Field. The 7,000-seat stadium was built in 1995.

Maryland jumped straight into the elite soon after forming its varsity team in 1946. In the opening game of the 1947 season, the Terrapins visited Temple, which had won 19 straight games. Maryland ended Temple's streak with a 3–1 win. That year, the Terrapins finished 6–0–1. The NCAA did not have a tournament at the time, but Maryland was recognized as the nation's No. 1 team.

Original coach Doyle Royal stayed with the Terrapins through the 1960s. He led Maryland to national runner-up finishes in 1960 and 1962. The Terrapins reached the final again in 1968. After two extra time periods, Maryland and Michigan State were tied 2–2. The game was declared a tie, and the teams were named co-champions.

Royal left in 1973. Maryland struggled for the next two decades. After finishing winless in ACC play in 1992, the school hired Sasho Cirovski as coach. Cirovski's team won only three games in 1993, but he quickly turned around the program.

After several winning seasons, Maryland put it all together in 2005. The Terrapins finished a 19–4–2 season by beating New Mexico 1–0 in the College Cup final. Maryland added another championship in 2008 and then a fourth in 2018 after joining the Big Ten Conference.

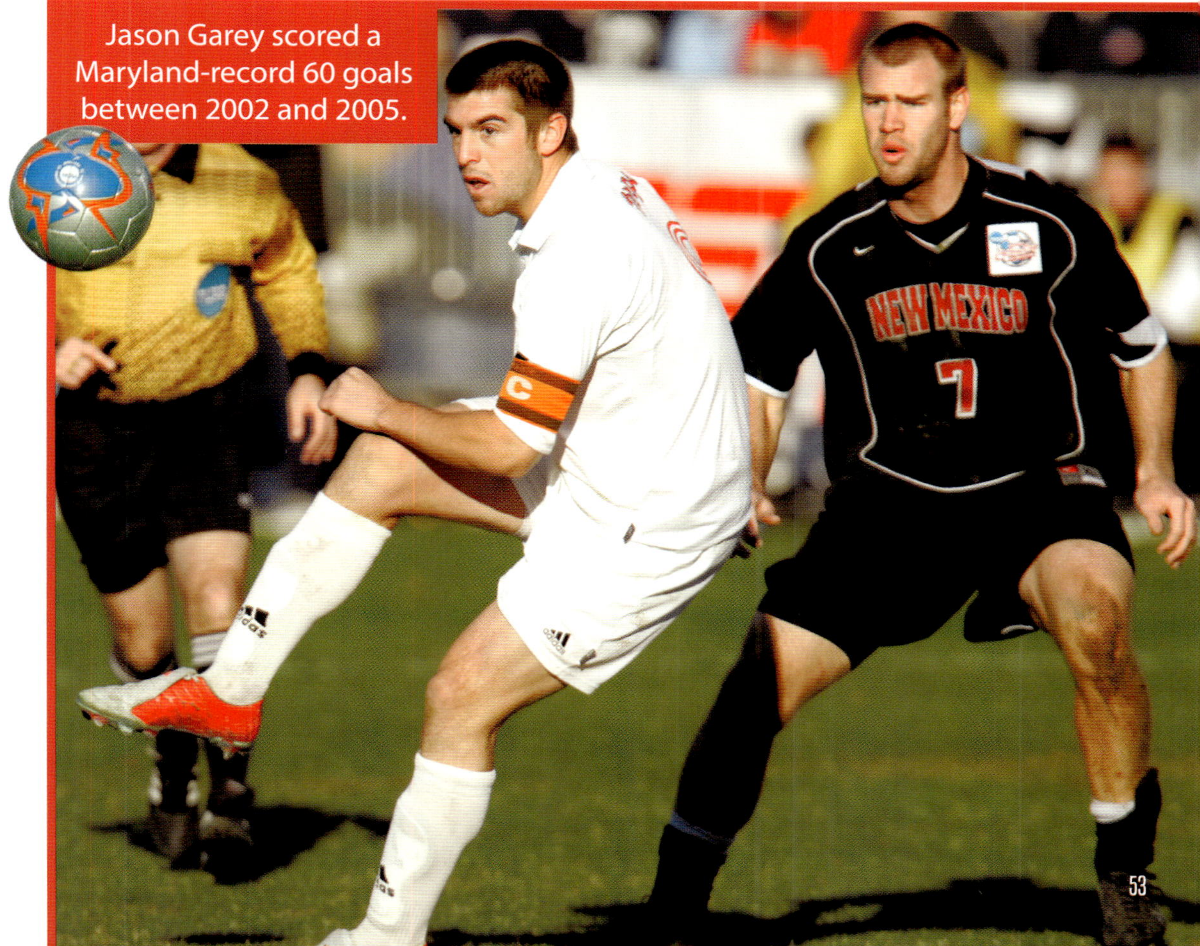

Jason Garey scored a Maryland-record 60 goals between 2002 and 2005.

Under Cirovski, the Terrapins have also become one of the best talent-producing programs in the country. In 2022, midfielder Ben Bender became Maryland's third No. 1 overall pick in the MLS college draft when he was taken by Charlotte FC. That same year, former Terrapins goalkeeper Dayne Saint Clair was named to Canada's team for the World Cup. He became the sixth Maryland player under Cirovski to take part in the tournament.

Maryland coach Sasho Cirovski, *center*, celebrates with his players after beating Akron for the 2018 NCAA title.

DOUBLE TROUBLE

In 2013, Maryland forward Patrick Mullins became just the seventh player to win the MAC Hermann Trophy two years in a row. Mullins won the 2012 award after scoring 17 goals. He topped that with 19 in 2013. Mullins is second all-time in scoring at Maryland behind Jason Garey, the only other Terrapin to win the MAC Hermann Trophy. Garey took home the hardware in 2005.

FACT BOX

First Season: 1946

Location: College Park, Maryland

Stadium: Ludwig Field

Conference: Big Ten Conference

All-Time Record: 779–373–129

NCAA Tournament Appearances: 43

College Cup Appearances: 14

National Titles: 1968, 2005, 2008, 2018

Top Coaches: Doyle Royal (1946–73); Sasho Cirovski (1993–)

Top Players: Cliff Krug (1958–60); Eberhard Klein (1962–64); Giancarlo Brandoni (1967–68); Sumed Ibrahim (1999–2003); Abe Thompson (2000–04); Jason Garey (2002–05); Zac MacMath (2008–10); Patrick Mullins (2010–13)

Mascot: Testudo

MICHIGAN STATE SPARTANS

Michigan State emerged as a soccer power during the 1960s. Led by coach Gene Kenney, the team went to six College Cups in seven years from 1962 to 1968. The Spartans took fourth place in the 1962 tournament. They then finished as runners-up in both 1964 and 1965 before a third-place finish in 1966.

Trevor Harris scored 23 goals in 1967 while leading Michigan State to a shared national championship.

Michigan State took on Saint Louis in the 1967 final. The field was drenched in rain, and players struggled to find their footing. After Michigan State star Guy Busch slipped and fell into one of the goalposts, the game was called. The two teams were declared co-champions.

The Spartans made it back to the title game in 1968 to face Maryland. Michigan State's Tony Keyes gave his team a 1–0 lead in the first half before the Terrapins scored twice. With less than ten minutes left, Michigan State's Frank Morant scored his first

Michigan State's Ken Krolicki, *right*, fires a pass against Maryland in a 2014 game.

goal of the season to tie the game 2–2. Neither team scored in two extra time periods, and once again Michigan State shared a national title.

Goalkeeper Joe Baum stopped eight shots in the 1968 final. In 1978, he became Michigan State's coach. Though Baum's

Midfielder Fatai Alashe was taken fourth overall in the 2015 MLS college draft after a distinguished four-year career at Michigan State.

teams were mostly successful, he didn't reach the NCAA Tournament until 2001. At that point, Michigan State had missed the tournament for 32 consecutive years.

The Spartans had to wait even longer to get back to the College Cup. Michigan fell in the Elite Eight of the NCAA Tournament three times in five seasons from 2013 to 2017. In 2018, forward Ryan Sierakowski scored twice in a 2–1 Elite Eight victory over James Madison to reach the national semifinals. There, the Spartans fell 5–1 to Akron.

THE STREAK

Michigan State goalkeeper Avery Steinlage went nearly a year without allowing a goal. Steinlage kept his net clean from October 15, 2008, to September 20, 2009. The NCAA-record shutout streak spanned 1,318 minutes and 26 seconds.

FACT BOX

First Season: 1956

Location: East Lansing, Michigan

Stadium: DeMartin Stadium

Conference: Big Ten Conference

All-Time Record: 633–368–128

NCAA Tournament Appearances: 20

College Cup Appearances: 7

National Titles: 1967, 1968

Top Coaches: Gene Kenney (1956–69); Joe Baum (1978–2008); Damon Rensing (2009–)

Top Players: Reiner Kemeling (1960–62); Mabricio Ventura (1960–62); Guy Busch (1965–67); Tony Keyes (1966–68); Trevor Harris (1967–69); Doug DeMartin (2005–08); Zach Bennett (2012–15)

Mascot: Sparty

NORTH CAROLINA TAR HEELS

North Carolina's David Stokes, *right*, battles for a loose ball in the 2001 NCAA championship game against Indiana.

The North Carolina men's team is sometimes overshadowed by the school's dominant women's program. But the men's team has its own strong history of success. The men's team was founded by coach Marvin Allen in 1947. Through 2024, North Carolina had endured only five losing seasons.

The Tar Heels first reached the College Cup in 1987. They beat rivals Duke and South Carolina in the early rounds of the NCAA Tournament but ultimately lost to Clemson in the semifinals. Under coach Elmar Bolowich, North Carolina remained strong throughout the 1990s. The Tar Heels finally broke through in 2001.

Their road to the national title game was filled with thrilling finishes. North Carolina beat American University 1–0 in extra time in the second round. The Tar Heels then needed three extra time periods to beat Fairleigh Dickinson in the Sweet 16. They rallied from down 2–0 to win 3–2.

In the College Cup semifinals, North Carolina beat Stanford

THE COACH

Anson Dorrance is more famous for coaching North Carolina's women's soccer dynasty. But Dorrance began coaching the North Carolina men in 1977. Two years later, when the university added a women's team, Dorrance coached both the men and women. He took the men's team to the 1987 College Cup. After the following season, he left the men's job.

North Carolina midfielder Enzo Martinez holds up the NCAA championship trophy after the Tar Heels' victory in 2011.

3–2, this time in four extra time periods. The Tar Heels then faced powerhouse Indiana in the final. Behind goals from Ryan Kneipper and Danny Jackson, North Carolina won 2–0 for its first national title.

Bolowich left North Carolina after the 2010 season. Carlos Somoano took over the Tar Heels. He led the team to a 21–2–3 record in his first season. North Carolina again faced a handful of dramatic games on its way to the College Cup final. The Tar Heels beat Indiana 1–0 in extra time in the second round. North Carolina's

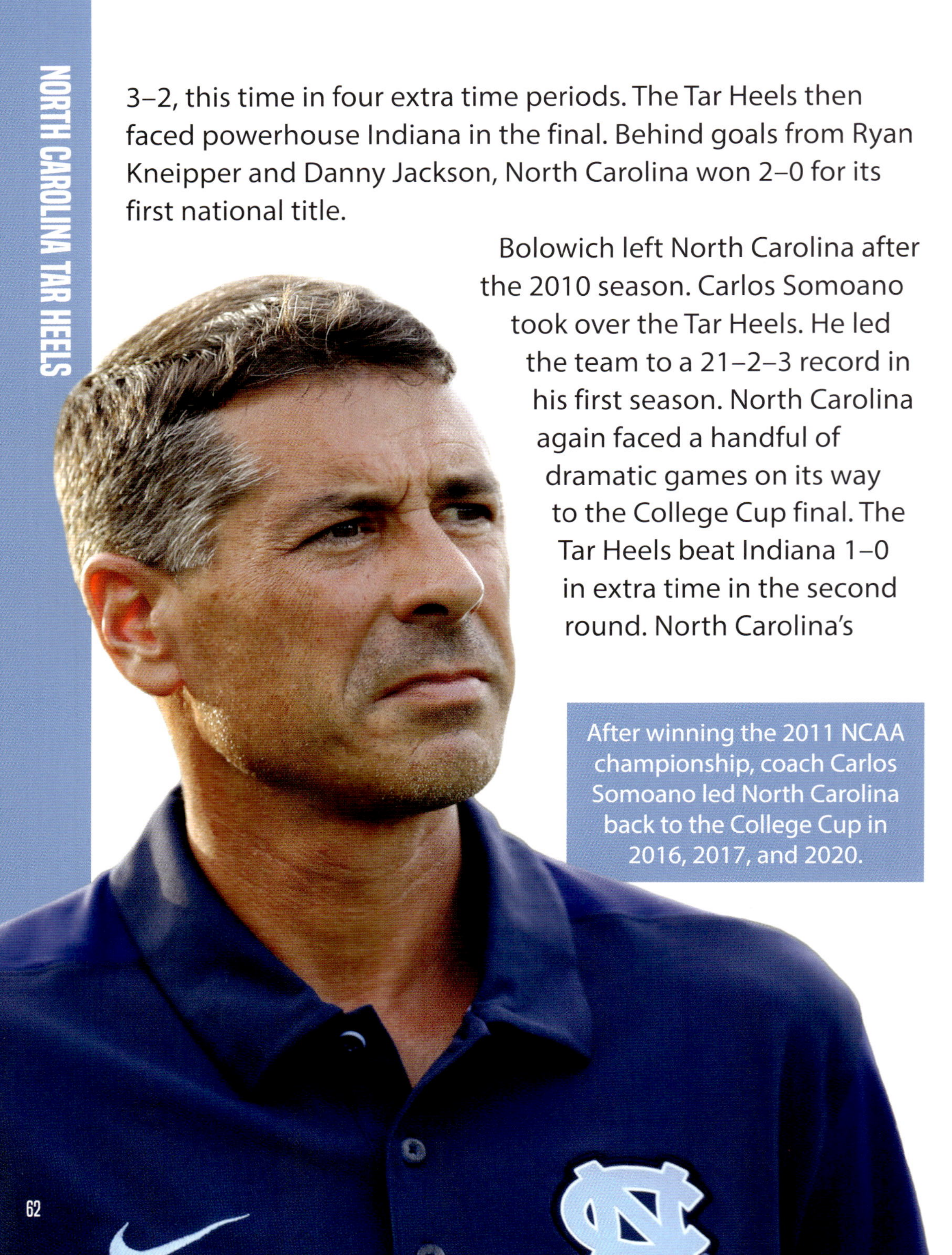

After winning the 2011 NCAA championship, coach Carlos Somoano led North Carolina back to the College Cup in 2016, 2017, and 2020.

semifinal game against UCLA was still tied 2–2 after extra time. Junior forward Ben Speas converted the deciding penalty kick to win the game. He then scored the only goal in a 1–0 win over Charlotte in the championship game.

Somoano became just the second coach to win a national championship in his first season. It was the start of a successful run. In 2024, the Tar Heels reached the NCAA tournament for the 13th time in his 14 seasons.

FACT BOX

First Season: 1947

Location: Chapel Hill, North Carolina

Stadium: Dorrance Field

Conference: Atlantic Coast Conference

All-Time Record: 810–362–134

NCAA Tournament Appearances: 31

College Cup Appearances: 9

National Titles: 2001, 2011

Top Coaches: Anson Dorrance (1977–88); Elmar Bolowich (1989–2010); Carlos Somoano (2011–)

Top Players: Derek Missimo (1987–90); Gregg Berhalter (1991–93); Temoc Suarez (1993–96); Carey Talley (1994–97); Chris Carrieri (1998–2000); Michael Farfan (2009–10); Boyd Okwuonu (2011–14); Cam Lindley (2016–17)

Mascot: Rameses

Notre Dame forward Joseph Lapira had seven multi-goal games during his MAC Hermann Trophy season in 2006.

Notre Dame joined the NCAA ranks in 1977, and the Fighting Irish made up for their lost years by winning right away. They won at least 12 games every year until 1985. Three years later, Notre Dame reached its first NCAA Tournament.

Despite that success, the Fighting Irish had never advanced past the second round when coach Bobby Clark took over in 2001. Under Clark's leadership, Notre Dame cleared that hurdle in 2005. A year later, junior forward Joseph Lapira posted an NCAA-best 50 points and 22 goals on the way to becoming the program's first MAC Hermann Trophy winner. His play helped the Fighting Irish reach the Elite Eight.

After several more years of frustration, Notre Dame entered the 2013 NCAA Tournament as a serious contender. The Fighting Irish outscored their first three opponents 10–3 to reach the College Cup for the first time. Midfielder Patrick Hodan scored both goals in a 2–0 semifinal win over New Mexico. Notre Dame then took on Maryland in the final.

The two teams had shared the ACC title and tied their regular-season matchup. Notre Dame fell behind with

A GOOD START

Notre Dame tied its first-ever game 3–3 against Dayton on September 16, 1977. Three days later, the Fighting Irish lost 2–0 against Saint Francis. Notre Dame then won every game until October 3, 1978. The school's 25-game winning streak tied an NCAA record previously set by Navy in 1964 and 1965.

The Fighting Irish celebrate after winning the 2013 College Cup over Maryland.

ten minutes left in the first half. But forward Leon Brown tied the game up before the halftime whistle. Less than ten minutes into the second half, captain Andrew O'Malley scored a header off a free kick to give Notre Dame a 2–1 lead. The Fighting Irish shut Maryland down the rest of the way to earn their first national title.

Clark left the program in 2017. Former Fighting Irish star Chad Riley took over. He led the team to the College Cup after the 2021 and 2023 seasons. In 2021, Notre Dame fell in the semifinals. Two years later, the Irish lost to Clemson in the national championship game.

Coach Chad Riley, *left*, led Notre Dame to the ACC championship in 2021.

FACT BOX

First Season: 1977

Location: Notre Dame, Indiana

Stadium: Alumni Stadium

Conference: Atlantic Coast Conference

All-Time Record: 602–295–120

NCAA Tournament Appearances: 23

College Cup Appearances: 3

National Titles: 2013

Top Coaches: Rich Hunter (1977–83); Dennis Grace (1984–89); Bobby Clark (2001–17)

Top Players: Kevin Lovejoy (1978–80); Richard Herdegen (1981–84); Greg Dalby (2003–06); Joseph Lapira (2004–07); Matt Besler (2005–08); Harrison Shipp (2010–13); Jack Lynn (2018–21); Bryan Dowd (2020–23)

Mascot: Leprechaun

PITTSBURGH PANTHERS

Pittsburgh, which is also known as Pitt, began its men's soccer program in 1954. The team went to the NCAA Tournament in both 1962 and 1965 under coach Leo Bemis. But the Panthers lost their opening game each time.

Pittsburgh was a long way from the NCAA Tournament in 2016. The program had not had a winning season since 2000. Program legend Joe Luxbacher was let go as coach. His replacement, Jay Vidovich, had previously coached Wake Forest to a national title. Vidovich had losing records in his first three seasons at Pittsburgh, but the team put things together in 2019. The Panthers had a winning record and qualified for the NCAA Tournament for the first time in 54 years. They added to the historic season by winning 2–0 against Lehigh in the first round for their first tournament win.

A year later, the Panthers won a program-record 16 games. They routed both Monmouth and Central Florida in the first two rounds of the NCAA Tournament. The Panthers then faced Washington in the Elite Eight. Pittsburgh was already up 2–0 late in the game

Pittsburgh coach Jay Vidovich finished the 2024 season with 347 career wins.

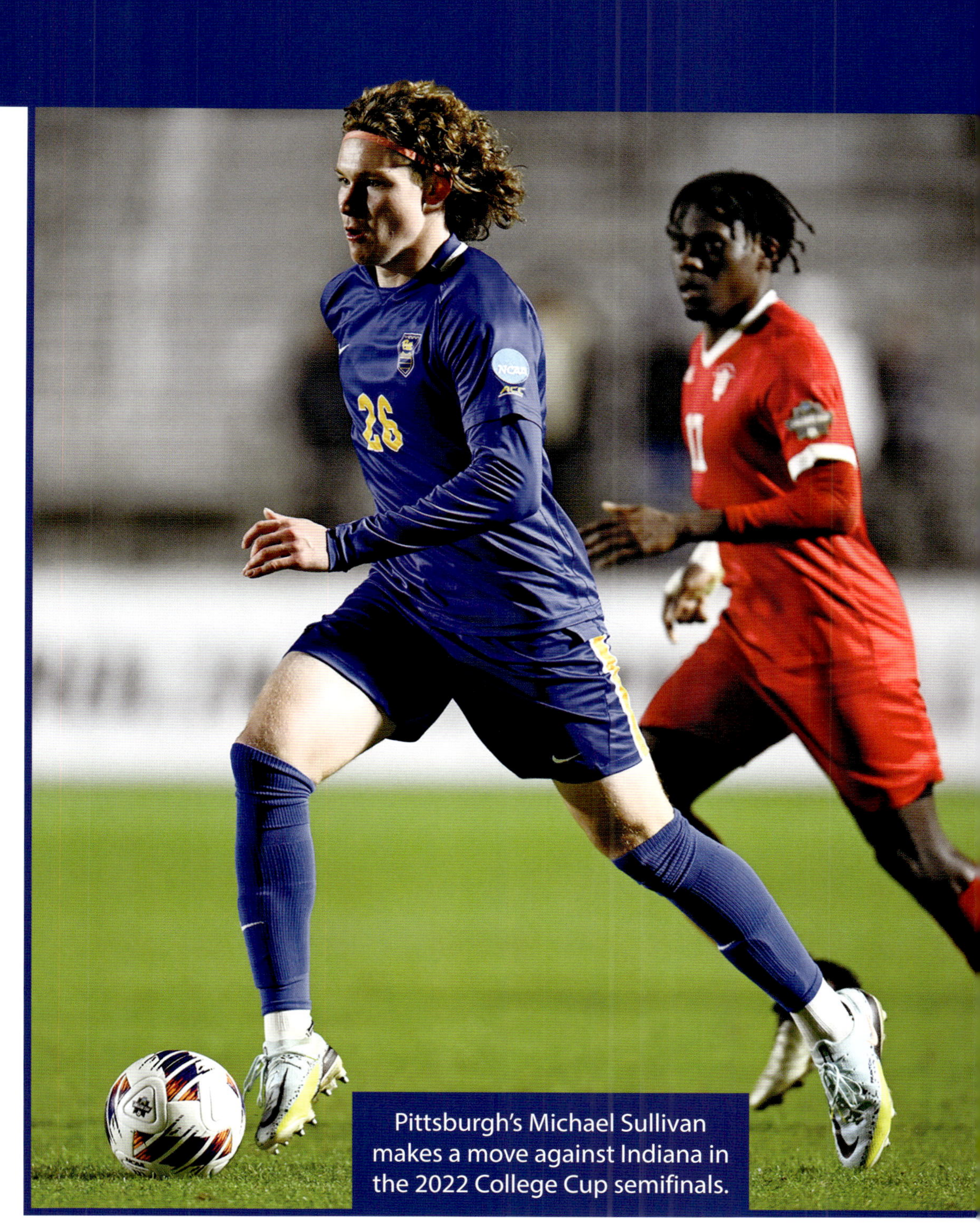

Pittsburgh's Michael Sullivan makes a move against Indiana in the 2022 College Cup semifinals.

Pittsburgh midfielder Valentin Noel, *right*, tries to stave off a North Carolina defender during a 2022 game.

when midfielder Veljko Petkovic beat the Huskies' goalkeeper from 40 yards. The win clinched Pittsburgh's first trip to the College Cup.

The Panthers lost to Indiana in the semifinals. But Vidovich continued the team's successful growth. In 2022, Pittsburgh once again reached the Elite Eight after wins against Cleveland State, Akron,

LONG-TERM EMPLOYMENT

The Panthers have had only three head coaches in school history. Leo Bemis coached from 1954 to 1983. He was replaced by Joe Luxbacher, who coached for 32 seasons. Current coach Jay Vidovich was hired in 2016.

and No. 1–ranked Kentucky. The Panthers then battled Portland into a second extra time period. Valentin Noel headed in a cross to send Pittsburgh to the College Cup for the second time in three years.

Once again, the Panthers fell to Indiana in the semifinals. But Pittsburgh continued to thrive under Vidovich. In 2024, the Panthers qualified for their sixth consecutive NCAA Tournament.

FACT BOX

First Season: 1954

Location: Pittsburgh, Pennsylvania

Stadium: Ambrose Urbanic Stadium

Conference: Atlantic Coast Conference

All-Time Record: 482–506–115

NCAA Tournament Appearances: 8

College Cup Appearances: 2

National Titles: None

Top Coaches: Leo Bemis (1954–83); Jay Vidovich (2016–)

Top Players: Joe Luxbacher (1971–73); Edward Kizza (2017–19); Veljko Petkovic (2019–21); Valentin Noel (2019–22); Jasper Löeffelsend (2020–21); Bertin Jacquesson (2020–22); Filip Mirkovic (2020–23)

Mascot: ROC the Panther

SAINT LOUIS BILLIKENS

A student waves a Saint Louis flag at Hermann Stadium prior to a Billikens game in 2021.

In 1958, Saint Louis University graduate Bob Guelker approached the school about starting a men's soccer team. The university gave him $200 to fund the program. After one year as a club team, the Billikens moved up to varsity status in 1959. The team was made up almost entirely of Saint Louis natives. The city had long been a hotbed of soccer culture in the United States, and the roster proved to be a winner. The Billikens won the first NCAA Tournament that season.

Guelker stayed with the school through the 1966 season and built the program into a dominant force. The Billikens won four more titles under his watch. Guelker's teams were high-scoring. Although Saint Louis fell short of the championship in 1964, the team set a record by averaging more than six goals per game.

In 1950, five Saint Louis natives had helped the United States earn a shocking upset over England in the World Cup. One of them was Harry Keough. He replaced Guelker as the Billikens' coach in 1967 and kept the dynasty going.

The Billikens shared the 1967 title after the championship game against Michigan State was abandoned due to weather. Saint Louis was back on top by itself in 1969. It beat San Francisco 4–0 in the title game.

Brian McBride set a Saint Louis record with 72 career goals from 1990 to 1993 before becoming a standout with the USMNT.

A BIG NAME IN SOCCER

Saint Louis's men's and women's teams play their home games in Hermann Stadium. It was named after Bob Hermann, a Saint Louis–based businessman who was a pioneer in promoting soccer in the United States. The MAC Hermann Trophy, given each year to the best player in men's and women's soccer, is also named after Hermann.

Saint Louis reached the Elite Eight of the 2021 NCAA Tournament. It was the team's deepest playoff run since 2003.

The win was the start of an incredible run. Between 1969 and 1973, Saint Louis went 74–5–7 while outscoring opponents 276–56. Billikens players swept the MAC Hermann Trophy all five years. Al Trost and Mike Seerey won the award twice, and Dan Counce earned it once. Saint Louis took home four championships in that stretch as well.

Fifty years later, the Billikens had not won another title. But Saint Louis is still one of the sport's most successful teams. Indiana won its eighth title in 2012. But the Hoosiers were still two short of the Billikens' record of ten.

FACT BOX

First Season: 1959

Location: Saint Louis, Missouri

Stadium: Hermann Stadium

Conference: Atlantic 10 Conference

All-Time Record: 841–280–132

NCAA Tournament Appearances: 51

College Cup Appearances: 16

National Titles: 1959, 1960, 1962, 1963, 1965, 1967, 1969, 1970, 1972, 1973

Top Coaches: Bob Guelker (1959–65); Harry Keough (1966–82); Joe Clarke (1983–96)

Top Players: Carl Gentile (1963–65); Pat McBride (1963–65); Al Trost (1968–70); Mike Seerey (1969–72); Dan Counce (1970–73); Brian McBride (1990–93); Matt McKeon (1992–95); Robert Kristo (2011–14)

Mascot: Billiken

STANFORD CARDINAL

Stanford's Seyi Abolaji holds off a UCLA defender during the 2002 College Cup final.

Stanford is one of the oldest college programs in Division I soccer. The program was founded in 1911. The team won six University and Club Soccer League championships in its first 11 seasons. But Stanford didn't become a contender in the NCAA Tournament era until the 1990s.

After finishing as national runners-up in 1998 and 2002, the Cardinal finally reached the top of the sport in the 2010s. Under coach Jeremy Gunn, Stanford built a powerful, defensive-minded team. In 2015, the Cardinal allowed only 12 regular-season goals and finished 14–2–2. After a pair of 3–1 wins to open the NCAA Tournament, Stanford outlasted No. 1 Wake Forest 2–1 in the Elite Eight.

The Cardinal and Akron then played to a scoreless draw in the College Cup semifinals. After winning in a shootout, the

Cardinal completed their first championship run by routing Clemson 4–0. Forward Jordan Morris, that year's MAC Hermann Trophy winner, scored two goals.

Stanford repeated as champions in 2016 in dramatic fashion. The Cardinal reached the final after beating North Carolina in a shootout. Stanford and Wake Forest then played a scoreless championship game. Cardinal goalkeeper Andrew Epstein then stopped two shots to help his team prevail 5–4 in another shootout.

Stanford players mob goalkeeper Andrew Epstein (in purple) after the team's shootout victory in the 2016 College Cup final.

Stanford's Drew Skundrich, *left*, tackles the ball away from Indiana's Griffin Dorsey in the 2017 College Cup final.

A year later, the Cardinal allowed only nine goals in 23 games, and none in five NCAA Tournament games. Once again the championship game was close. Stanford and Indiana played into a second extra time period. With under eight minutes left, Stanford midfielder Sam Werner stole the ball in the Hoosiers' penalty area and hammered a shot just under the crossbar to win the title. Stanford became only the second team to capture three straight championships.

FACT BOX

First Season: 1911

Location: Stanford, California

Stadium: Laird Q. Kagan Stadium

Conference: Atlantic Coast Conference

All-Time Record: 800–530–216

NCAA Tournament Appearances: 22

College Cup Appearances: 7

National Titles: 2015, 2016, 2017

Top Coaches: Nelson Lodge (1976–83); Bobby Clark (1996–2000); Jeremy Gunn (2012–)

Top Players: Ted Rafalovich (1978–81); Willie Guicci (1979–81); Jorge Titinger (1980–83); Brandon Vincent (2012–15); Jordan Morris (2013–15); Foster Langsdorf (2014–17); Tomas Hilliard-Arce (2014–17); Tanner Beason (2016–19)

Mascot: The Tree (unofficial)

MILESTONE

The Cardinal squared off with UC Santa Barbara in the second round of the 2024 NCAA Tournament. After jumping to a 2–0 lead, Stanford allowed two goals in the second half. The Cardinal eventually won in a shootout. It was a milestone victory for the program. Stanford became the tenth Division I team to reach 800 all-time victories.

SYRACUSE ORANGE

Forward Ben Polk scored 12 goals for Syracuse in 2015.

For nearly a century, Syracuse was a struggling program. Founded in 1920, the team from central New York reached the NCAA Tournament just once, in 1984, before coach Ian

McIntyre arrived in 2010. The English-born coach quickly turned Syracuse into a contender in the ACC.

The Orange recorded their first tournament wins in 2012 and were seeded for the first time in 2014. Entering the 2015 tournament as the No. 6 seed, Syracuse advanced to the Elite Eight. Forward Ben Polk's header off a corner kick with just under 12 minutes remaining against Boston College sent the Orange to their first College Cup. Syracuse was knocked out in the semifinals in a shootout by ACC rival Clemson.

Syracuse returned to the tournament in 2016, 2018, and 2019. After a stumble in 2020 and 2021, Syracuse was not expected to contend in 2022. But McIntyre's team surprised the ACC and returned to the NCAA Tournament as the No. 3 seed. It survived three one-goal games to reach the College Cup again. In the semifinals against

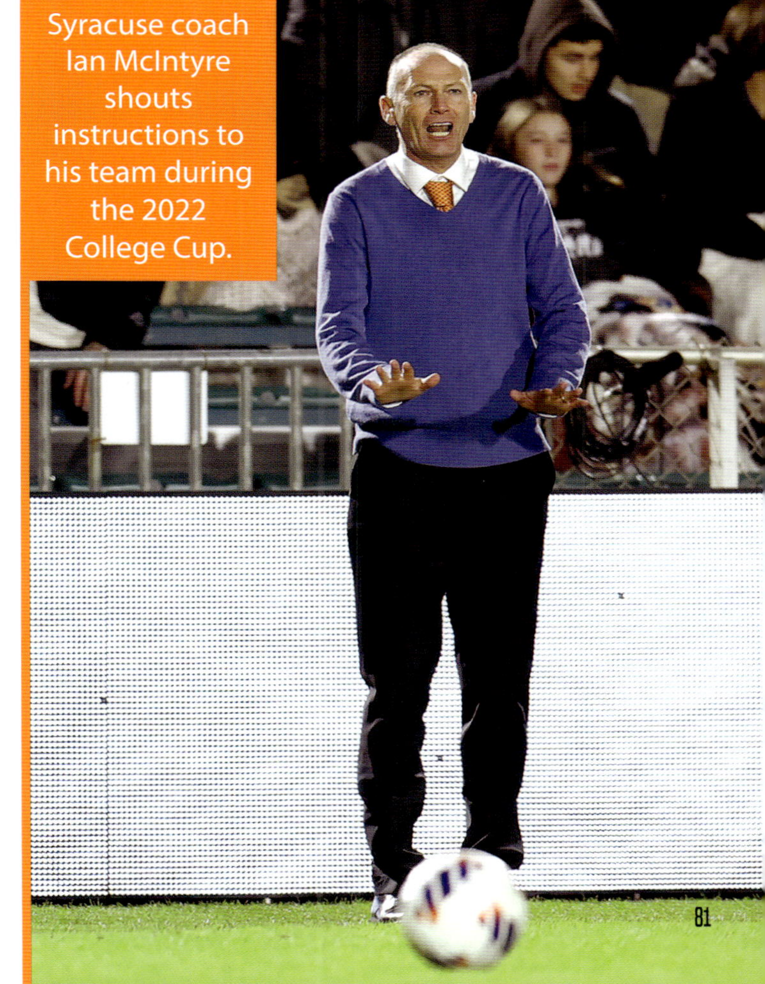

Syracuse coach Ian McIntyre shouts instructions to his team during the 2022 College Cup.

Creighton, Syracuse let two one-goal leads slip away. Finally, star forward Levonte Johnson's close-range finish late in the game propelled the Orange into the final with a 3–2 win.

In the championship game, Syracuse faced traditional power Indiana. Nathan Opoku and Curt Calov both scored in the first half as the Orange built a 2–1 lead. But the Hoosiers tied the game in the second half. After going scoreless through extra time, the teams went to a dramatic shootout. With the shootout tied 6–6, Syracuse goalkeeper Russell

Syracuse players hold up the championship trophy after beating Indiana in the 2022 College Cup.

Shealy stopped Indiana's shot. Captain Amferny Sinclair then fired home the winning kick to deliver the Orange their first national championship.

IMPORTED FROM CANADA

Syracuse is roughly 100 miles (161 km) from the Canadian border. Throughout its history, Syracuse's soccer team has fielded several Canadian stars. Defender Kamal Miller was a key piece of the Orange's 2015 College Cup team. Forward Levonte Johnson was a finalist for the 2022 MAC Hermann Trophy. Both Miller and midfielder Tajon Buchanan represented Canada at the 2022 World Cup in Qatar.

FACT BOX

First Season: 1920

Location: Syracuse, New York

Stadium: SU Soccer Stadium

Conference: Atlantic Coast Conference

All-Time Record: 550–550–143

NCAA Tournament Appearances: 9

College Cup Appearances: 2

National Titles: 2022

Top Coaches: Dean Foti (1991–2009); Ian McIntyre (2010–)

Top Players: John McEwan (1931–32); Vincent Black (1931–33); William Nelson (1950, 1952–53); Marcello Vitale (1979–82); Alex Bono (2012–14); Miles Robinson (2015–16); Levonte Johnson (2022)

Mascot: Otto the Orange

UCLA BRUINS

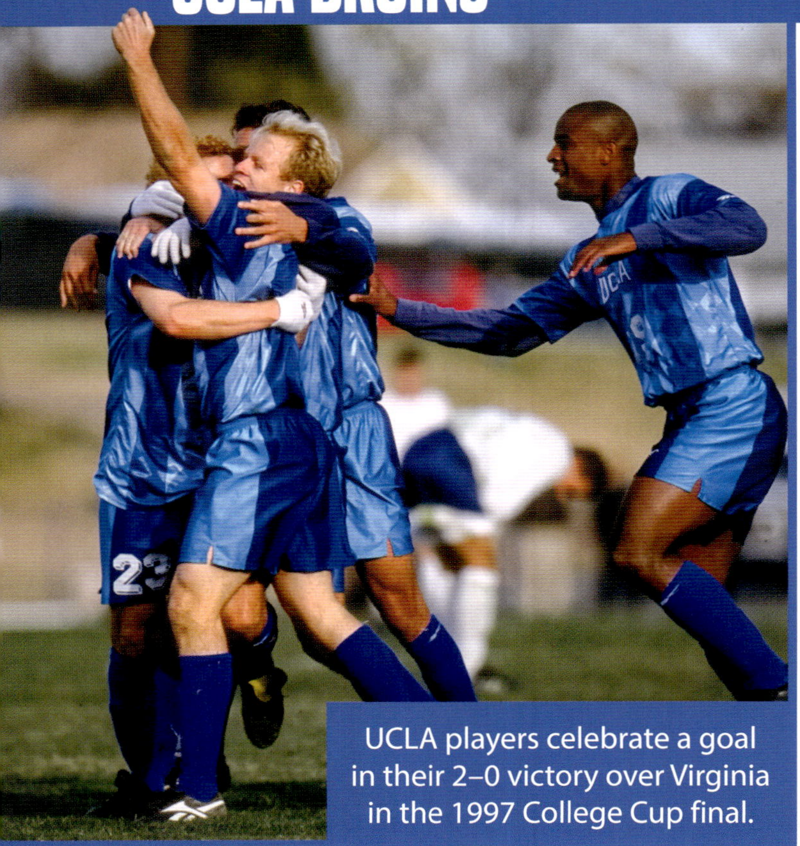

UCLA players celebrate a goal in their 2–0 victory over Virginia in the 1997 College Cup final.

No college men's soccer team has amassed more wins than UCLA's 1,027. When the Bruins passed the 1,000-victory mark in 2021, no other team had reached even 900 wins. From 1967 to 2006, the Bruins posted an NCAA-record 40 straight winning seasons.

That success didn't translate into championships right away. Coach Dennis Storer led the Bruins to College Cup championship games in 1970, 1972, and 1973. Each time, UCLA fell to fellow powerhouse Saint Louis. The Bruins also lost in the semifinals in 1974 and again in 1984 under coach Sigi Schmid.

UCLA finally put everything together in 1985. The Bruins allowed only two goals in five NCAA Tournament games. But the championship game against American University was still tied after seven extra time periods. Substitute defender Andy Burke, who had been injured most of the season, finally scored to end the marathon game after 166 minutes, 5 seconds and deliver the Bruins' first championship.

UCLA won again in 1990, allowing only one goal in four tournament games. The defense was anchored by future USMNT goalkeeper Brad Friedel. Friedel was the hero again in the final as the Bruins beat Rutgers in a shootout.

UCLA players celebrate their 2002 College Cup victory over Stanford.

UCLA added a third title in 1997. This time the Bruins beat Virginia 2–0 in the title game. In 2002, first-year head coach Tom Fitzgerald guided the Bruins to a fourth championship. They held off rival Stanford 1–0 in the championship game.

The Bruins returned to the College Cup final again in 2006 and 2014. However, they fell short each time. In the latter season, German-born midfielder Leo Stolz became the second UCLA man to win the MAC Hermann Trophy. Friedel had been the first, in 1992.

Over the years, UCLA has also built a tradition of producing stars for both MLS clubs and the USMNT. Over MLS's first 28 seasons, no school sent more players to the league than

Paul Caligiuri starred for UCLA from 1982 to 1986 before playing professionally in Europe and for the USMNT.

UCLA's 82. Meanwhile, former Bruins such as Paul Caligiuri, Cobi Jones, and Friedel became all-time greats with the USMNT. In total, 15 UCLA players had taken part in a World Cup with the United States through 2022. And every US World Cup team between 1990 and 2010 had at least three former UCLA players on its roster.

SCORING IN BUNCHES

In a 2016 game against Akron, the Bruins set an NCAA record for the fastest three goals. Abu Danladi scored twice in a span of 11 seconds early in the second half. Blayne Martinez added a third goal 21 seconds later. It was only the third time that a team had scored three goals in under a minute.

FACT BOX

First Season: 1937

Location: Los Angeles, California

Stadium: Wallis Annenberg Stadium

Conference: Big Ten Conference

All-Time Record: 1,027–308–142

NCAA Tournament Appearances: 49

College Cup Appearances: 14

National Titles: 1985, 1990, 1997, 2002

Top Coaches: Dennis Storer (1967–73); Sigi Schmid (1980–98)

Top Players: Ole Mikkelson (1977–80); Paul Caligiuri (1982–86); Cobi Jones (1988–91); Chris Henderson (1989–90); Brad Friedel (1990–92); Sasha Victorine (1996–99); Carlos Bocanegra (1997–99); Leo Stolz (2012–14)

Mascot: Joe and Josephine Bruin

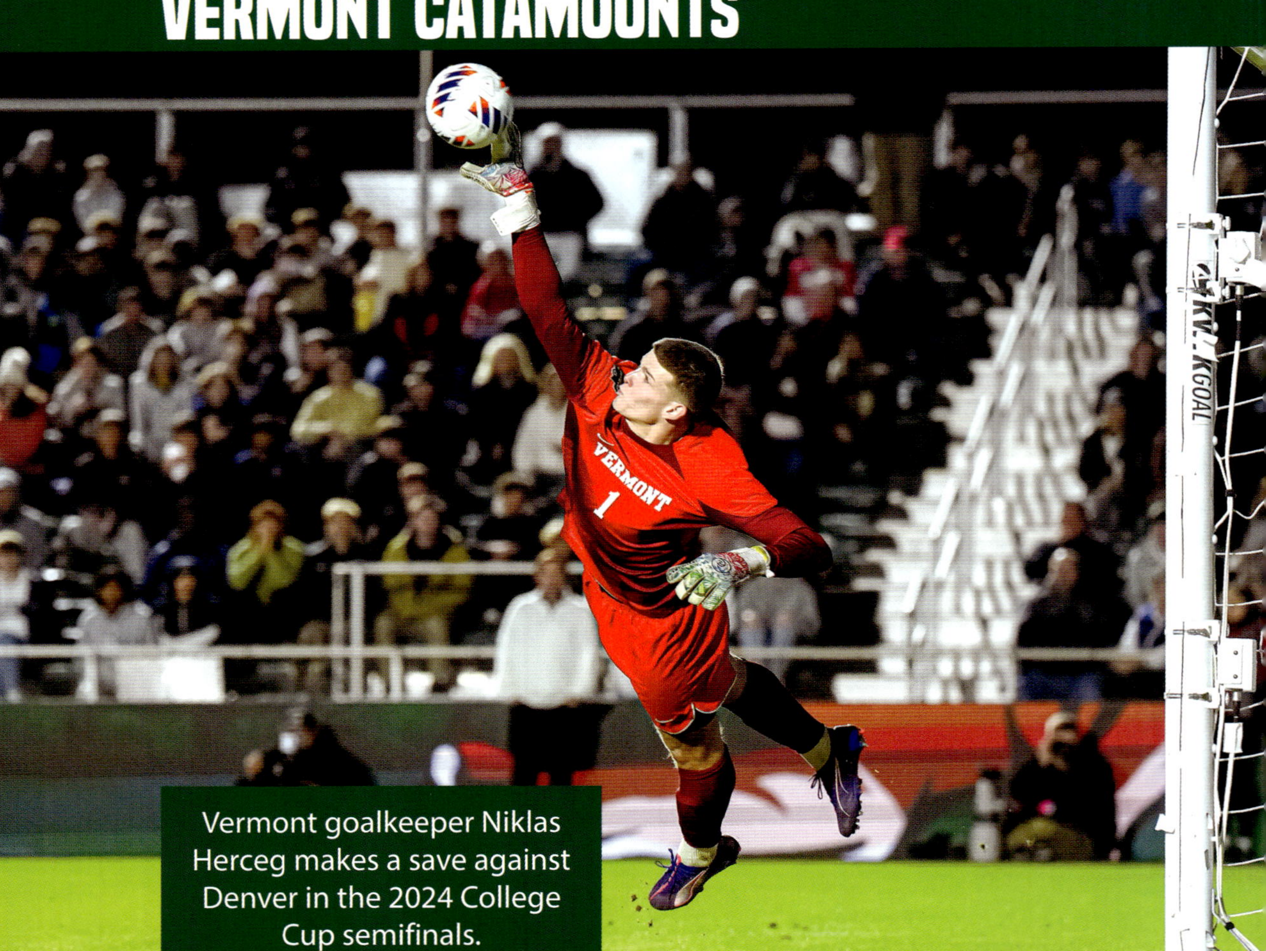

Vermont goalkeeper Niklas Herceg makes a save against Denver in the 2024 College Cup semifinals.

Vermont's men's soccer program began playing in 1964. For decades, the Catamounts were a strong program in small conferences. The team played in the Yankee Conference until 1979. After eight years as an independent, Vermont then joined the America East Conference in 1988.

After winning a program-record 19 games in 1989, the Catamounts made their first NCAA Tournament appearance. Led by the scoring of Mike Mason, Vermont made a surprise run to the Elite Eight. The Catamounts went back to the tournament in 1990 under longtime coach Ron McEachen but lost in the first round.

Vermont didn't make another deep tournament run until 2022. Coach Rob Dow's team once again reached the Elite Eight. The Catamounts entered the 2024 season convinced they could win a national title. The team even had a replica NCAA Tournament trophy made. The players carried it with them all season.

Catamounts forward Yaniv Bazini scored in every NCAA Tournament game except the final in 2024.

A CHAMPIONSHIP FIRST

The men's soccer team made Vermont history when it won the 2024 NCAA title. It marked the school's first national title in a sport outside of downhill skiing. Vermont's ski team had won six national titles.

Vermont entered the tournament ranked No. 17 in the country and was not given a seed. After beating Iona 5–0 in the first round, the Catamounts needed a late goal to beat No. 7 Hofstra. Vermont then beat San Diego in extra time and earned the nickname "Cardiac Cats."

Captains Zach Barrett, *left*, and Adrian Schulze Solano hold up the national championship trophy after Vermont's extra time win against Marshall in the 2024 College Cup final.

The Catamounts beat tournament-favorite Pittsburgh in the Elite Eight to reach the College Cup. Vermont then faced Denver in the semifinals. The Catamounts trailed 1–0 with only minutes to play. But star midfielder Yaniv Bazini scored the tying goal. Vermont ultimately won in a shootout.

In the championship game against Marshall, the Catamounts rallied again. The teams entered extra time tied 1–1 before Vermont forward Maximilian Kissel scored the game-winning goal. The Catamounts became the first unseeded team to win the College Cup since UC Santa Barbara in 2006.

FACT BOX

First Season: 1964

Location: Burlington, Vermont

Stadium: Virtue Field

Conference: America East Conference

All-Time Record: 531–371–132

NCAA Tournament Appearances: 14

College Cup Appearances: 1

National Titles: 2024

Top Coaches: Ron McEachen (1985–95); Rob Dow (2017–)

Top Players: John Koerner (1974–77); Mike Mason (1986–89); Jim St. Andre (1986–89); Brian Wright (2013–16); Alex Nagy (2018–22); Yaniv Bazini (2022–24)

Mascot: The Catamount

Maximilian Kissel scores Vermont's game-winning goal in extra time of the 2024 College Cup final.

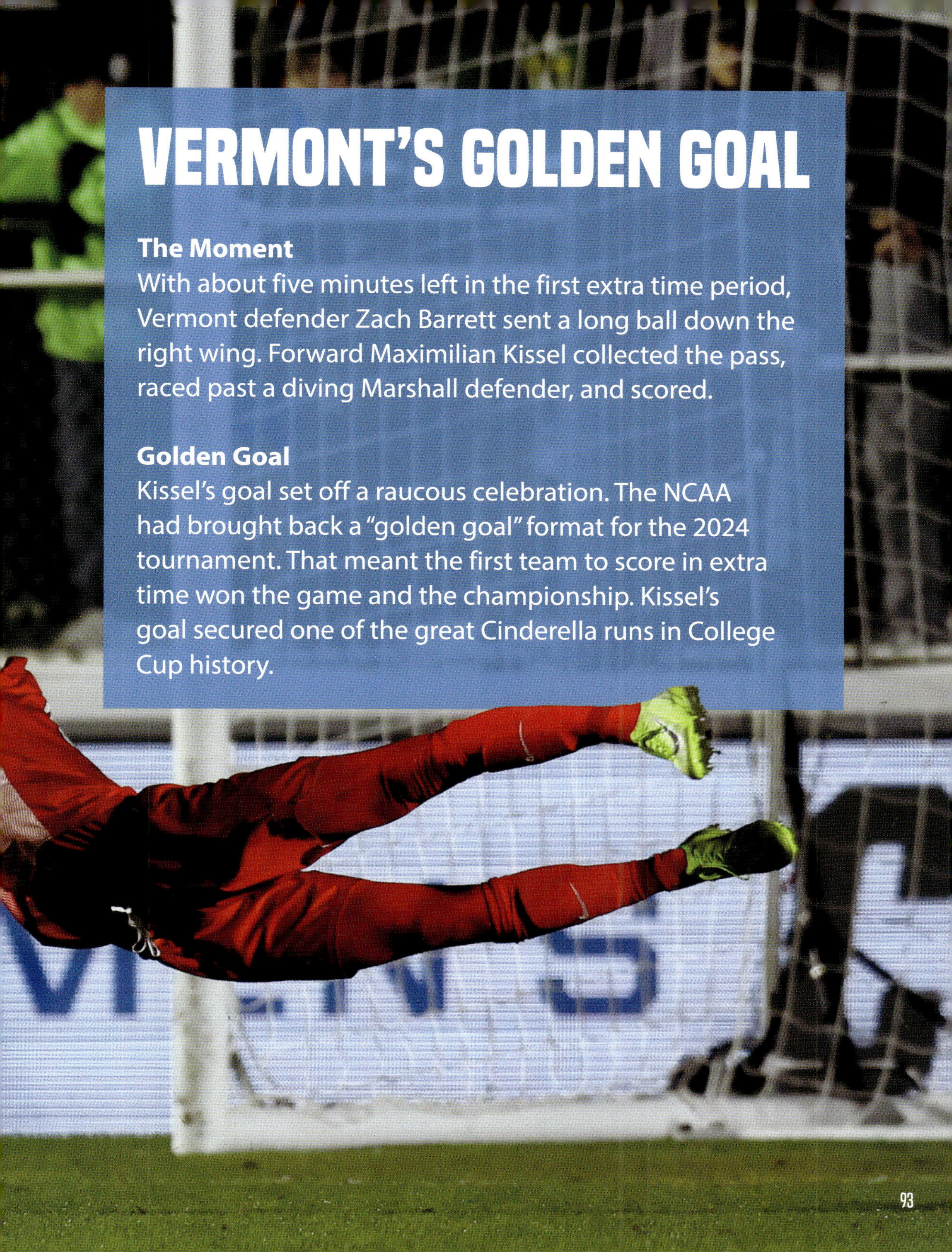

VERMONT'S GOLDEN GOAL

The Moment

With about five minutes left in the first extra time period, Vermont defender Zach Barrett sent a long ball down the right wing. Forward Maximilian Kissel collected the pass, raced past a diving Marshall defender, and scored.

Golden Goal

Kissel's goal set off a raucous celebration. The NCAA had brought back a "golden goal" format for the 2024 tournament. That meant the first team to score in extra time won the game and the championship. Kissel's goal secured one of the great Cinderella runs in College Cup history.

VIRGINIA CAVALIERS

Virginia's men's soccer team debuted in 1941. It finished 0–9 that season. But over the next several decades, the Cavaliers grew into a college soccer power.

By the late 1980s, Virginia was one of the nation's elite teams. The program was led by Bruce Arena, who would go on to coach the USMNT. A handful of Virginia's players, such as midfielder John Harkes and goalkeeper Tony Meola, became standouts for the USMNT as well.

Virginia appeared in its first College Cup final in 1989 and shared the title with Santa Clara. Two years later, in 1991, the Cavaliers started the greatest championship run in men's college soccer. Once again facing Santa Clara in the NCAA championship game, Virginia prevailed in a shootout. The hero was backup goalkeeper Tom Henske. Arena substituted Henske for starter Jeff Causey just before the shootout. Henske made two saves to seal the win.

In addition to coaching soccer, Bruce Arena also coached Virginia's men's lacrosse team from 1978 to 1985.

Virginia players pile on after defeating Akron in a shootout to win the 2009 College Cup.

In 1992, Virginia outscored its four NCAA Tournament opponents 12–1. The Cavaliers sealed a second straight championship with a 2–0 win over San Diego. Led by future USMNT star Claudio Reyna, Virginia beat South Carolina 2–0 to win the 1993 title.

No team had ever won four consecutive championships. The Cavaliers were not expected to repeat with Reyna having left

the team. After some early struggles, however, the team got hot and made it back to the 1994 College Cup. Virginia outlasted Rutgers 2–1 in the semifinals. That set up a title game against another college soccer power, Indiana.

Midway through the first half, Virginia star A. J. Wood slipped the ball past Indiana's goalie. The Cavaliers hung on to win 1–0. After the game, Wood and Virginia's three other seniors were recognized as the sport's

Virginia's Jake Rozhansky dribbles against UCLA in the 2014 College Cup final. After a scoreless draw, Virginia won the game 4–2 in a shootout.

first four-time NCAA champions. Virginia went 84–9–4 during those four years.

Arena left after the 1995 season. New coach George Gelnovatch guided the team to additional championships in 2009 and 2014. With seven championships, Virginia trailed only Indiana and Saint Louis on the all-time list.

CO-CHAMPIONS

Virginia and Santa Clara squared off for the national championship in freezing conditions in 1989. At the time, teams played 30 minutes of extra time, but there were no shootouts. Since the teams were still tied 1–1 at the end of extra time, both were declared champions. It was the third time in College Cup history that two teams had shared the title. It was also the last. The next year, the rules were changed to include shootouts in championship games.

FACT BOX

First Season: 1941

Location: Charlottesville, Virginia

Stadium: Klöckner Stadium

Conference: Atlantic Coast Conference

All-Time Record: 837–386–142

NCAA Tournament Appearances: 44

College Cup Appearances: 13

National Titles: 1989, 1991, 1992, 1993, 1994, 2009, 2014

Top Coaches: Bruce Arena (1978–95); George Gelnovatch (1996–)

Top Players: Jeff Gaffney (1982–85); John Harkes (1985–87); Tony Meola (1988–89); Claudio Reyna (1991–93); A. J. Wood (1991–94); Mike Fisher (1993–96); Ben Olsen (1995–97); Alecko Eskandarian (2000–02)

Mascot: Cavman

WAKE FOREST DEMON DEACONS

Wake Forest's Marcus Tracy had 13 goals and 10 assists in 2007.

Wake Forest started its men's soccer program in 1980, after many of its ACC rivals were already well established. But the Demon Deacons quickly became contenders in the powerful soccer conference. Wake Forest won its first conference tournament title in 1989, beating Duke in a shootout. That same season, the Demon Deacons won an NCAA Tournament game for the first time.

By the 2000s, Wake Forest was a regular at the NCAA Tournament. The Demon Deacons reached their first College Cup in 2006. A year later, MAC Hermann Trophy winner Marcus Tracy led Wake Forest on another tournament run. In the Elite Eight, Tracy recorded an assist on the winning goal in a 1–0 extra time victory over Notre Dame. The forward then scored both Wake Forest goals in a 2–0 win over Virginia Tech in the semis.

Wake Forest players celebrate after beating Ohio State in the 2007 College Cup final.

The Demon Deacons faced Ohio State for the championship. The game was a physical contest, with 37 fouls and six yellow cards between the teams. After falling behind 1–0 at halftime, Wake Forest rallied. Tracy scored from the center of the penalty area in the 66th minute to tie the game. He then set up fellow attacker Zack Schilawski for the game-winner eight minutes later.

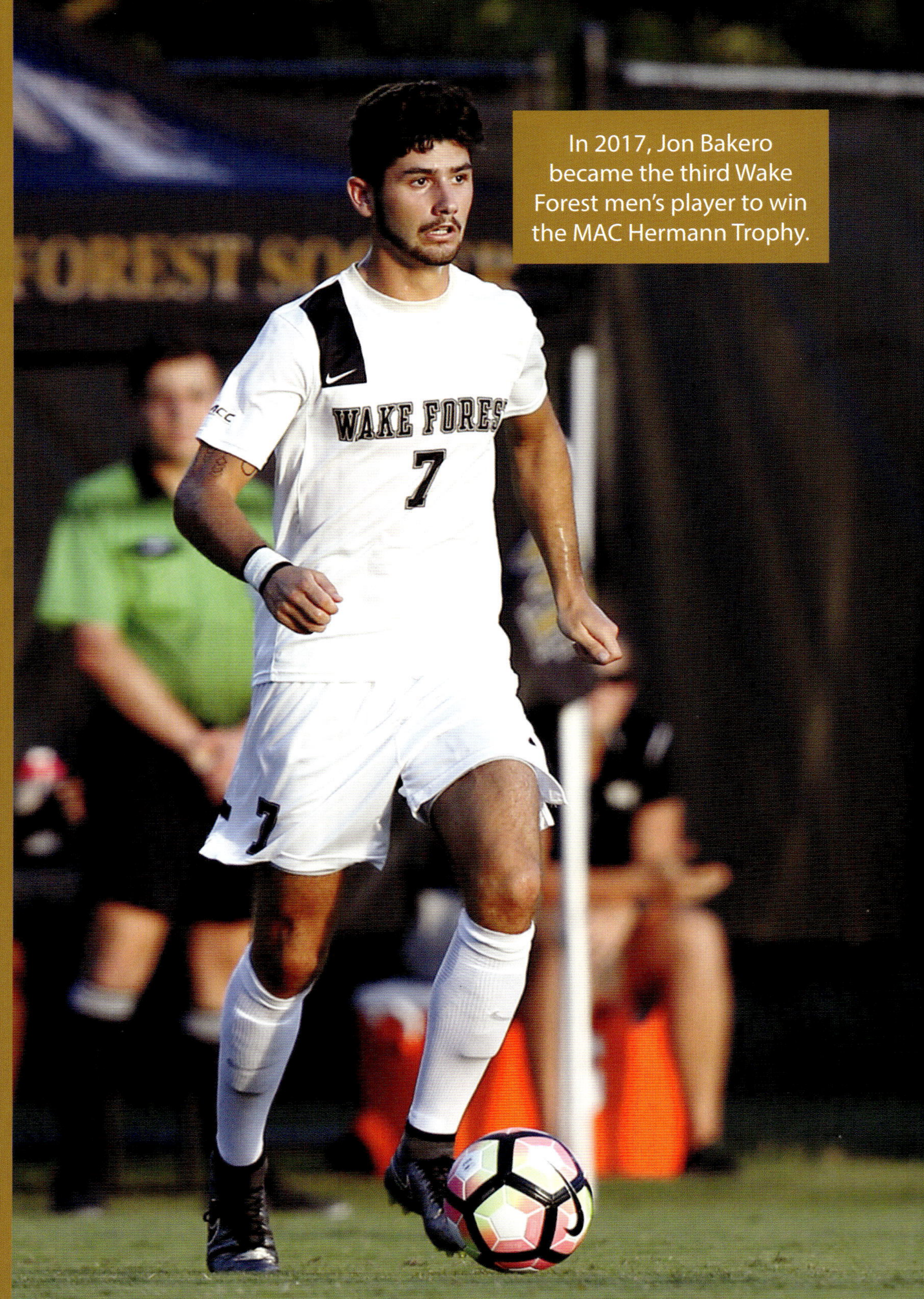

In 2017, Jon Bakero became the third Wake Forest men's player to win the MAC Hermann Trophy.

SAVING THE DAY

Wake Forest owed much of its early success to goalkeeper Jose Grave de Peralta. In four seasons from 1980 to 1983, Grave de Peralta stopped an NCAA-record 620 shots. He is one of only two Division I goalkeepers with more than 600 career saves. Wake Forest had three winning records in that time and finished 45–31–10 in Grave de Peralta's career.

The win was part of a stretch of four straight College Cup appearances for Wake Forest. The Demon Deacons fell in the semifinals in both 2008 and 2009. The team returned to the championship game in 2016 led by MAC Hermann Trophy winner Ian Harkes. In the semifinals, Wake Forest beat Denver in the second extra time period on a goal by Harkes. However, the Demon Deacons fell to Stanford in a shootout during the championship game.

FACT BOX

First Season: 1980

Location: Winston-Salem, North Carolina

Stadium: Spry Stadium

Conference: Atlantic Coast Conference

All-Time Record: 565–272–110

NCAA Tournament Appearances: 28

College Cup Appearances: 6

National Titles: 2007

Top Coaches: Jay Vidovich (1994–2014); Bobby Muuss (2015–)

Top Players: Mark Erwin (1980–83); Scott Sealy (2001–04); Sam Cronin (2005–08); Zack Schilawski (2006–09); Ike Opara (2007–09); Marcus Tracy (2005–08); Ian Harkes (2013–16); Jon Bakero (2014–17)

Mascot: The Demon Deacon

WOMEN'S TEAMS
BYU COUGARS

As of 2025, Jennifer Rockwood (in black hat) was still the only head coach in BYU women's soccer history.

Jennifer Rockwood studied at Brigham Young University (BYU) during the late 1980s. With no varsity women's soccer team at the time, Rockwood played on the school's club team. Eventually she began coaching that team and making its travel arrangements. So when BYU decided to start a varsity team in 1995, Rockwood applied to be the coach. Not only did she get the job but she still held it 30 years later.

Rockwood quickly built the Cougars into one of the nation's consistently strong teams. They finished 22–1 in their second season. By their third season, the Cougars reached the NCAA Tournament. Over the next 28 seasons, BYU missed the tournament only three times. Within those tournaments, the team made the Sweet 16 nine times. Five of those teams got to the Elite Eight.

BYU's most successful season came in 2021. After a 17–5–2 regular season, the No. 4 seed Cougars caught fire in the NCAA Tournament. They outscored opponents 15–2 over four wins

BYU's Jamie Shepherd takes on a Florida State defender during the 2021 College Cup final.

to open the tournament. That included a 1–0 victory over No. 1 seed Virginia in the Sweet 16.

Competing in their first College Cup, the Cougars battled Santa Clara to a 0–0 draw on the Broncos' home field. BYU finally won in a shootout to set up a title-game showdown against the tournament's overall top seed, Florida State. Once again, neither team could score through 110 minutes of regulation or extra time. In the shootout, BYU goalkeeper Cassidy Smith made a big stop. But Florida State's goalkeeper made two, giving the Seminoles a 4–3 shootout win.

Two years later, in 2023, BYU joined the Big 12 Conference. No team scored more goals than the Cougars that season. Once again they got to the College Cup. But this time BYU fell 2–0 to Stanford in the semifinals.

Over the years, BYU's South Field has attracted some big crowds. Having a lot of local players helps. The Cougars' 2021 NCAA runner-up squad had 24 of 30 players from Utah, including 9 of the 11 starters. As BYU is affiliated with the Church of Jesus Christ of Latter-day Saints, also known as the Mormons, most of the players are also members of the church.

OLYMPIC STAR

Shauna Rohbock scored a BYU-record 95 goals in the late 1990s. With limited options for playing soccer after college, she took up bobsledding. Rohbock and teammate Valerie Fleming qualified for the 2006 Winter Olympics in Turin, Italy, where they won a silver medal. Rohbock also raced at the 2010 Winter Olympics in Vancouver.

The Cougars are a popular team in their hometown of Provo, Utah.

FACT BOX

First Season: 1995

Location: Provo, Utah

Stadium: South Field

Conference: Big 12 Conference

All-Time Record: 464–136–62

NCAA Tournament Appearances: 25

College Cup Appearances: 2

National Titles: None

Top Coach: Jennifer Rockwood (1995–)

Top Players: Shauna Rohbock (1995–98); Erika Woodbury (2004–07); Lindsi Lisonbee Cutshall (2009–12); Ashley Hatch (2013–16); Mikayla Colohan (2017–21); Jamie Shepherd (2019–23); Laveni Vaka (2019–23); Brecken Mozingo (2020–23)

Mascot: Cosmo the Cougar

CALIFORNIA GOLDEN BEARS

The women's soccer team at California debuted by going 6–0 in 1982. That set up a successful start for the team sometimes known as Cal. From 1983 to 1988, the Golden Bears made five NCAA Tournaments in six seasons. Three of those teams reached the College Cup.

Bill Merrell set the foundation. After the team played without school funding in 1982, he took over the next year and began building up support. Merrell stayed just three years in his first stint. During that time, the Bears reached their first NCAA Tournament (1983) and College Cup (1984).

Oski has been California's mascot since 1941.

Jean Paul Verhees also had a short run as coach, staying for 1987 and 1988. California made the College Cup both years. The 1987 team didn't lose all season until the semifinals against defending champion North Carolina. California fell in the semifinals the next year, too.

California forward Alex Morgan (13) battles with Stanford's Allison Falk during a 2008 game.

A new era of success began soon after Kevin Boyd took over as coach in 1997. From 1998 to 2006, his teams made the NCAA Tournament in all but one year. In the middle of that run, star forward Laura Schott became California's all-time leading scorer with 56 goals. However, the Bears got past the second round of the tournament only once under Boyd.

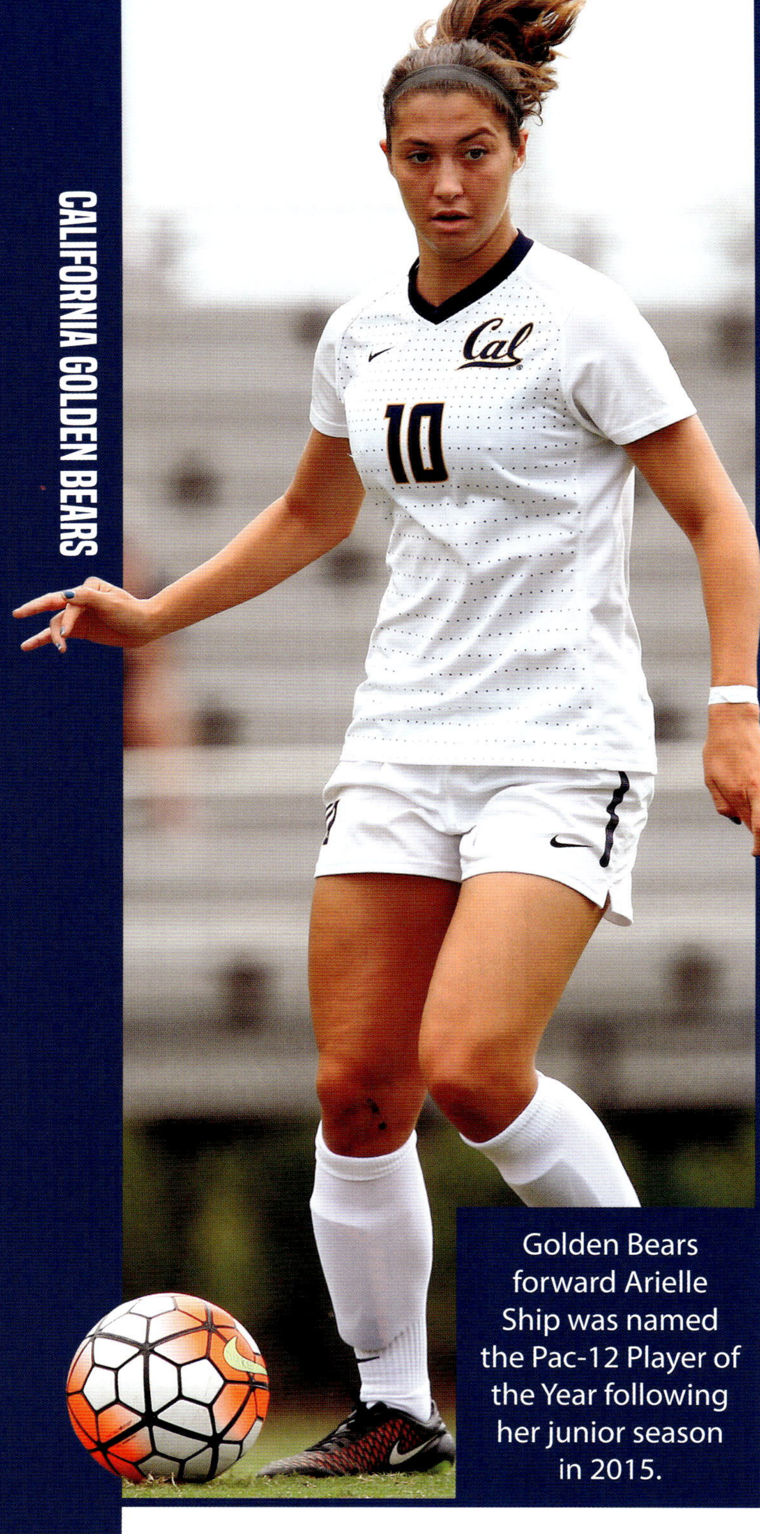

Golden Bears forward Arielle Ship was named the Pac-12 Player of the Year following her junior season in 2015.

Future USWNT superstar Alex Morgan arrived in 2007. Among her 45 career goals were five hat tricks. She was named a first team All-American as a senior in 2010. However, even she couldn't end California's streak of early exits in the NCAA Tournament.

The Golden Bears made the NCAA Tournament 14 straight seasons from 2004 to 2017. Yet California made it past the second round only once in that span. In seven of those tournaments, the Golden Bears lost in the first round. The tournament streak ended in 2018 when

California went 5–12–2. That marked only the second losing season in team history.

California soon bounced back. However, a cloud formed over the program in 2020 when some players accused longtime coach Neil McGuire of abusive behavior. McGuire denied wrongdoing and remained the coach. The team returned to the NCAA Tournament in 2019, 2022, and 2024.

A GOLDEN CAREER

USWNT fans know Joy Fawcett as one of the team's all-time great defenders. A member of the team's "Fab Five," she played in 241 games for the national team from 1987 to 2004. That international career began while she was still at California and playing in an attacking role. The star then known as Joy Biefeld scored a team-record 23 goals as a sophomore in 1987. Her 55 total goals stood as a California record for many years as well.

FACT BOX

First Season: 1982

Location: Berkeley, California

Stadium: Edwards Stadium

Conference: Atlantic Coast Conference

All-Time Record: 484–251–93

NCAA Tournament Appearances: 28

College Cup Appearances: 3

National Titles: None

Top Coaches: Jean Paul Verhees (1987–88); Kevin Boyd (1997–2006); Neil McGuire (2007–)

Top Players: Lesle Gallimore (1982–85); Mary Harvey (1983–85); Joy Biefeld (1986–89); Valerie Pope (1987–90); Laura Schott (1999–2002); Alex Morgan (2007–10); Arielle Ship (2013–16); Indigo Gibson (2014–17)

Mascot: Oski

CLEMSON TIGERS

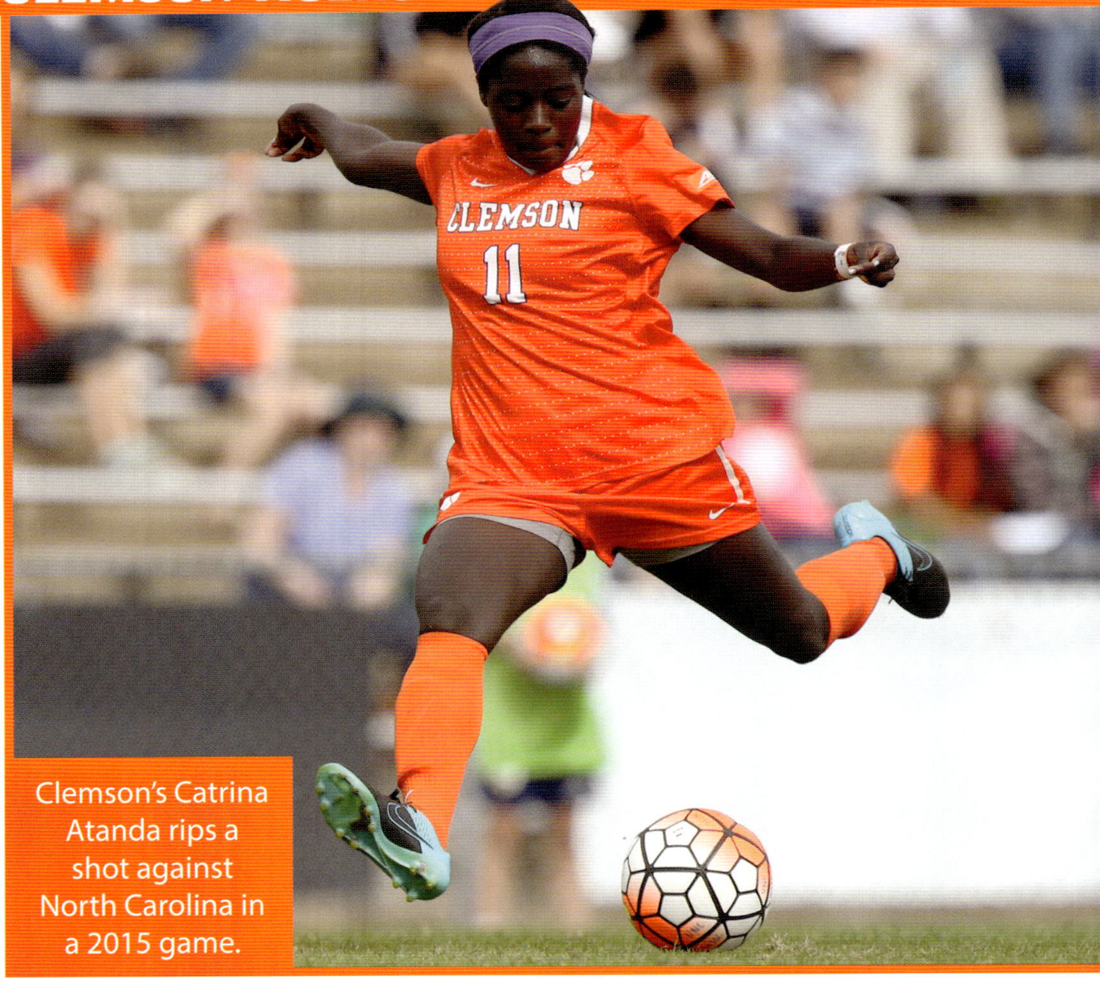

Clemson's Catrina Atanda rips a shot against North Carolina in a 2015 game.

When Clemson was starting its women's soccer team in 1994, the school hired Tracey Leone as coach. Before her second season, Leone identified star high school midfielder Sara Burkett as a potential star. Burkett bought into the coach's vision. Before long, she was the Tigers' first All-American.

Burkett's calm demeanor kept her teammates balanced. But she was a great playmaker as well. Behind Leone and

Burkett, the Tigers quickly developed into a competitive program. From 1994 to 2007, Clemson never missed an NCAA Tournament. With Burkett leading the way, the Tigers got to the Elite Eight in 1997.

In 1999, Tracey and her husband, Ray Leone, shared coaching duties. Ray took over as the lone head coach in 2000. Clemson reached the Elite Eight both seasons. Then Todd Bramble kept the NCAA Tournament streak going.

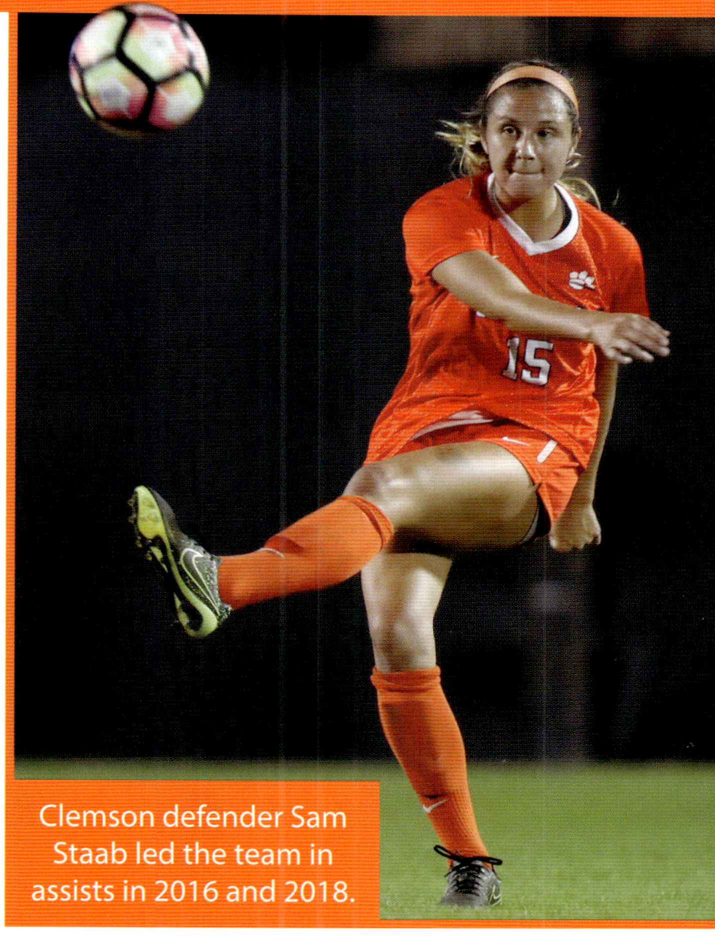
Clemson defender Sam Staab led the team in assists in 2016 and 2018.

The Tigers qualified in all seven of Bramble's seasons. The 2006 team got back to the Elite Eight. But when Bramble left for a new job after the 2007 season, Clemson took a step back. After making 14 straight NCAA Tournaments, the Tigers missed six in a row. Three of those teams went winless in ACC play.

Things began to turn around when Eddie Radwanski became coach in 2011. The coach began bringing in talented recruits. By 2014, the Tigers began a new streak of consecutive

Clemson's Dani Davis takes control of the ball against Florida State during the 2023 College Cup semifinals.

A COUPLE OF COACHES

As a player, Tracey Leone helped the USWNT win the first Women's World Cup in 1991. She later got into coaching. So did her husband, Ray Leone. Both applied for the Clemson job in 1994. Though Tracey got the job, both ended up coaching at the school. Each later went on to coach other college teams as well.

NCAA Tournament berths. Defender Sam Staab provided stability for the Tigers. As a senior in 2018 she was the ACC Defensive Player of the Year.

Though Clemson regularly qualified for the NCAA Tournament, deep runs were rare.

From 2014 to 2022, the Tigers advanced past the round of 32 only twice. The 2023 team proved different.

As a No. 1 seed, Clemson won its first two games. In the Sweet 16, goalkeeper Halle Mackiewicz made a key stop to help the Tigers get past Georgia in a shootout. Then Caroline Conti came up big in the Elite Eight. Her 84th minute goal secured a 2–1 win over Penn State and Clemson's first trip to the College Cup. The run finally ended with a 2–0 loss to Florida State in the semifinals. The good times didn't last, though. For the first time in 11 years, Clemson missed the NCAA Tournament in 2024.

FACT BOX

First Season: 1994

Location: Clemson, South Carolina

Stadium: Riggs Field

Conference: Atlantic Coast Conference

All-Time Record: 351–224–59

NCAA Tournament Appearances: 22

College Cup Appearances: 1

National Titles: None

Top Coaches: Tracey Leone (1994–99); Todd Bramble (2001–07); Eddie Radwanski (2011–)

Top Players: Sara Burkett (1995–98); Beth Keller (1996–99); Nancy Augustyniak (1997–2000); Julie Augustyniak (1997–2000); Deliah Arrington (1999–2002); Allison Graham (2002–05); Sam Staab (2015–18); Halle Mackiewicz (2020–23); Megan Bornkamp (2020–25)

Mascot: The Tiger and Tiger Cub

UConn's Kristen Graczyk (13) dribbles against North Carolina during the 2003 NCAA championship game.

Connecticut added two program-changing players ahead of its second season in 1980. Tara Buckley went on to earn All-America honors all four years while anchoring the Huskies' defense. Meanwhile, her sister, Moira Buckley, finished her career as the school's all-time leading scorer.

Before the 1981 season, the team better known as UConn brought in Len Tsantiris as coach. In his second season, the Huskies went undefeated in the regular season and qualified for the sport's first NCAA Tournament. As the top seed, they

made a run to the College Cup semifinals. Though Central Florida beat UConn there, the Huskies came back to win the third-place game against Missouri–Saint Louis.

That season established UConn as one of the top teams in the early NCAA era. The Huskies proved it by getting back to the College Cup in 1983 and 1984. The 1984 team reached the national title game before falling 2–0 to North Carolina. Six years later, the Huskies were back

The UConn Huskies have played at Joseph J. Morrone Stadium since their first season in 1979.

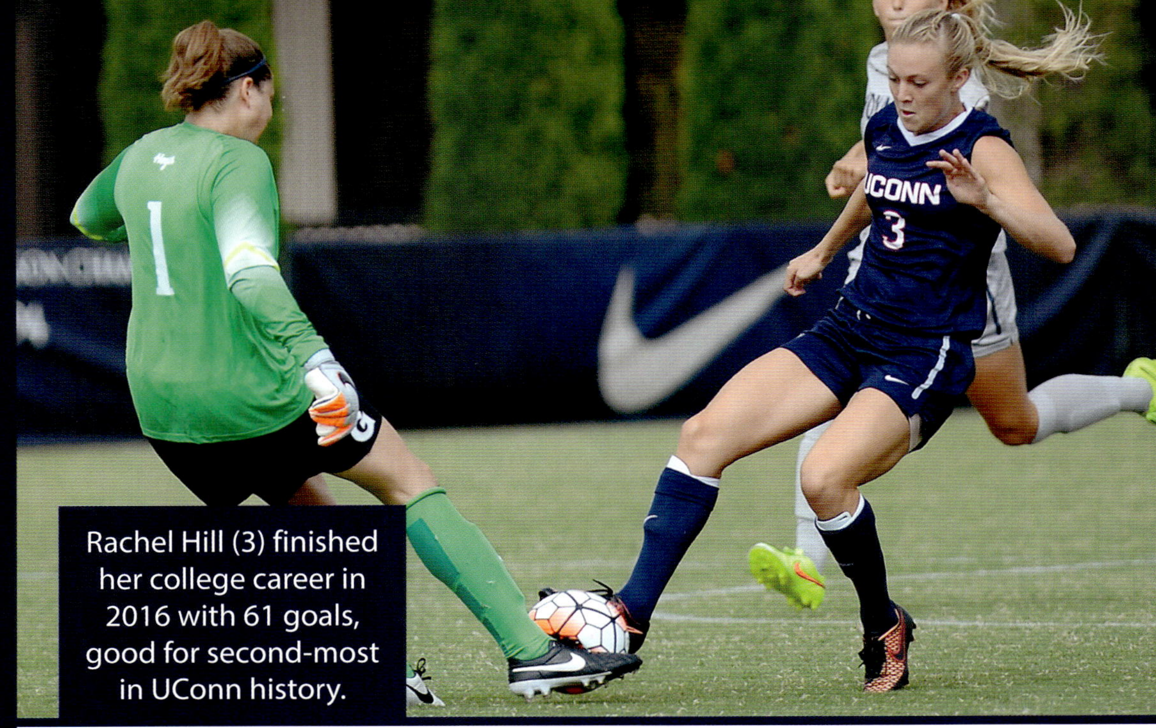

Rachel Hill (3) finished her college career in 2016 with 61 goals, good for second-most in UConn history.

in the 1990 title game. However, this time they fell 6–0 to the dominant Tar Heels.

The Big East Conference named UConn's Sara Whalen its 1995 and 1996 Defensive Player of the Year. Going into the 1997 season, Tsantiris wanted to improve the Huskies' offense. He moved Whalen to forward. She responded by scoring 21 goals and recording 22 assists. Whalen added five goals and three assists in the NCAA Tournament as the Huskies advanced all the way to the final. But once again, North Carolina beat UConn in the title game, this time 2–0.

Jessica Gjertsen and Kristen Graczyk sparked UConn's attack in 2003. The duo scored a combined total of seven goals during that year's NCAA Tournament. Their scoring slowed down in the championship game, though. For the fourth time, North Carolina ended UConn's title dreams in a 6–0 Tar Heels win.

Tsantiris led UConn to 26 straight NCAA Tournaments. When he retired after the 2017 season, Tsantiris had 570 wins, the second-most by any coach in the sport. Margaret Rodriguez took over. In 2024, she led the Huskies to the Big East Tournament title. That was the team's first conference tournament championship since 2016.

SHORT-LIVED RECORDS

While Sara Whalen earned many accolades in 1997, teammate Jen Carlson set a school record that year with 24 goals. A year later, freshman midfielder Mary-Frances Monroe matched that mark and added 17 assists. Her 65 points set the school record, surpassing Whalen's total from 1997.

FACT BOX

First Season: 1979

Location: Storrs, Connecticut

Stadium: Joseph J. Morrone Stadium

Conference: Big East Conference

All-Time Record: 629–249–77

NCAA Tournament Appearances: 32

College Cup Appearances: 8

National Titles: None

Top Coaches: Len Tsantiris (1981–2017)

Top Players: Tara Buckley (1980–83); Moira Buckley (1980–83); Kerry Connors (1993–96); Sara Whalen (1994–97); Jen Carlson (1997–2000); Mary-Frances Monroe (1998–2000); Kristen Graczyk (2001–04); Rachel Hill (2013–16)

Mascot: Jonathan the Husky

DUKE BLUE DEVILS

Duke coach Robbie Church won 311 games from 2001 to 2024.

Bill Hempen began coaching Duke during its first season in 1988. From the start, the Blue Devils were a winning team. In 1992, they nearly became national champions. In the team's first NCAA Tournament, Duke won three games to reach the final. However, once there the Blue Devils ran into a North Carolina team that some say was the best ever. The rival Tar Heels dominated Duke in a 9–1 win.

That season established Duke as a regular in the NCAA Tournament. Hempen led the Blue Devils to all but one tournament through 2000. They barely missed a beat when Robbie Church took over for Hempen in 2001. Through 2024, his teams reached 21 NCAA Tournaments. That included runs to the Sweet 16 or beyond in five of his first 13 seasons.

Duke's first College Cup run under Church came in 2011. Mollie Pathman scored two goals to lift the Blue Devils to a 4–1 win over Wake Forest in the semifinals. But Stanford beat Duke 1–0 in the championship game.

After missing out on the 2014 tournament, Duke returned in a big way in 2015. That year, goalkeeper E. J. Proctor stopped two shots in a shootout win over Stanford in the Elite Eight. Duke then beat defending champion Florida State in the semifinals before losing 1–0 to Penn State in the title game.

Proctor continued to anchor Duke's defense during the 2017 NCAA Tournament. The senior star didn't allow a goal on Duke's

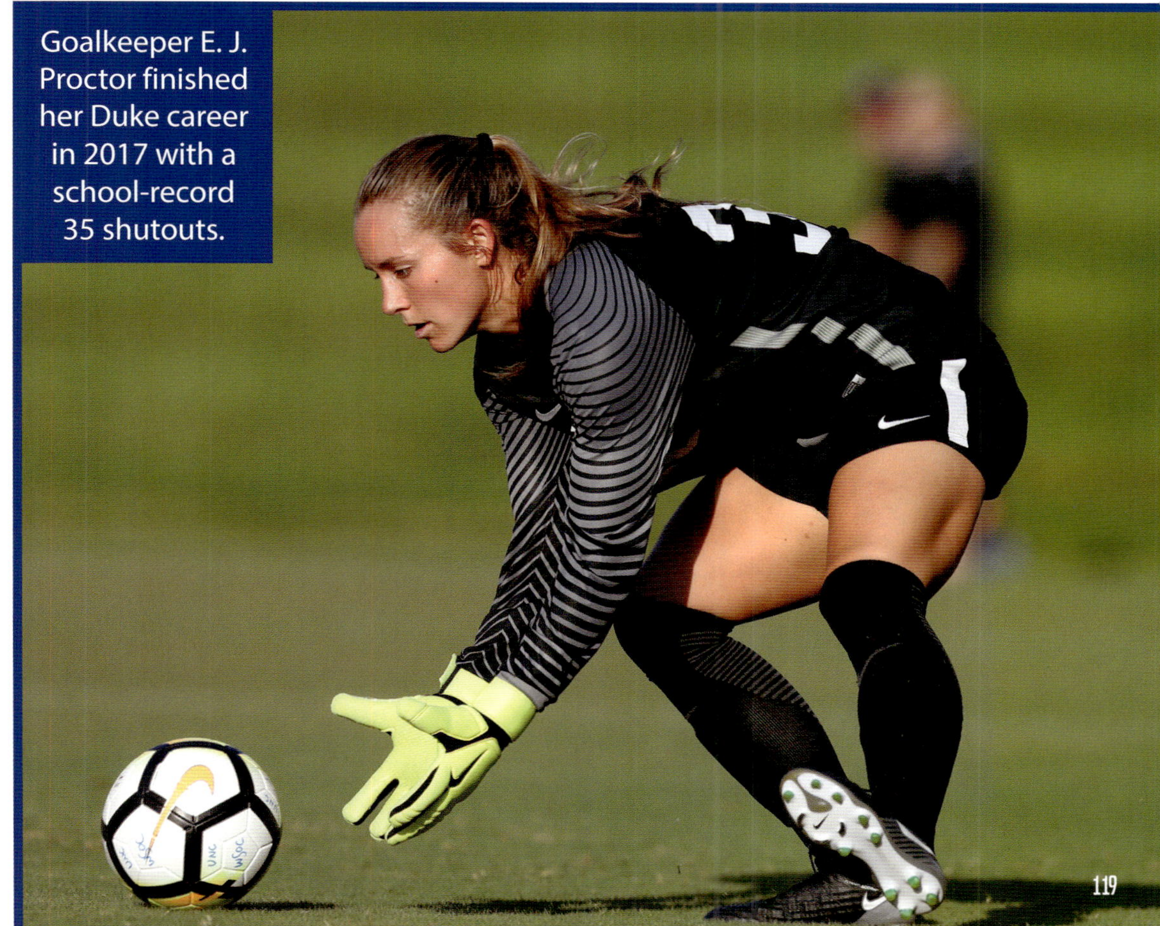

Goalkeeper E. J. Proctor finished her Duke career in 2017 with a school-record 35 shutouts.

Duke forward Michelle Cooper scored a school-record six NCAA Tournament goals in 2022.

CONSISTENT KELLY

Kelly Walbert added her name all over Duke's record book during the early 1990s. She left the team in 1995 with a team record 47 goals and 23 assists. Thirty years later, her goals record still stood. Her 18 goals in 1994 remained the single-season record until 2022. Walbert also started a team-record 90 consecutive games and became Duke's first three-time All-American.

run to the College Cup. In the semifinals against UCLA, Proctor secured another shutout. However, after the teams played to a 0–0 draw through extra time, the Bruins won in a shootout.

Michelle Cooper took college soccer by storm 2021. Her 12 goals set a school record for freshmen. Then she set the overall school record by scoring 19 goals the next year. Those scoring numbers helped Cooper become the first Duke player to win the MAC Hermann Trophy.

Before the 2024 season, Church announced he'd retire following his 24th year at Duke. The Blue Devils sent him off with a fourth trip to the College Cup. However, North Carolina ended Church's tenure with a 3–0 loss in the semifinals.

FACT BOX

First Season: 1988

Location: Durham, North Carolina

Stadium: Koskinen Stadium

Conference: Atlantic Coast Conference

All-Time Record: 473–250–83

NCAA Tournament Appearances: 29

College Cup Appearances: 5

National Titles: None

Top Coaches: Bill Hempen (1988–2000); Robbie Church (2001–24)

Top Players: Kelly Walbert (1992–95); Andi Melde (1994–97); Casey McCluskey (2001–04); Laura Weinberg (2010–13); E. J. Proctor (2014–17); Kayla McCoy (2015–18); Michelle Cooper (2021–22)

Mascot: The Blue Devil

FLORIDA GATORS

Becky Burleigh won SEC Coach of the Year honors four times with Florida from 1995 to 2021.

Under coach Becky Burleigh, Florida got off to a fast start as a program. In only their second season, the Gators won the 1996 SEC Tournament and qualified for the NCAA Tournament. That began a streak of six consecutive SEC titles and NCAA Tournament berths.

Danielle Fotopoulos was a big reason for Florida's success. In 1996, the sophomore forward scored a school-record 34 goals. After missing the 1997 season with a knee injury, Fotopoulos came back strong in 1998. Playing alongside star freshman forward Abby Wambach, Fotopoulos scored 32 goals. Behind their powerful attack, the Gators lost only one game in the regular season. It was a 2–1 extra time defeat to defending champion North Carolina.

Florida kept the momentum going in the NCAA Tournament. The Gators stormed through their opponents on the way to the championship game, a rematch with North Carolina. The Tar Heels had long dominated the sport. They came into the title game having won 46 straight games. Five minutes in, a North Carolina player fouled Fotopoulos just outside the penalty

Florida forward Danielle Fotopoulos left the school in 1998 as the NCAA's all-time leading scorer with 118 goals.

area. Fotopoulos blasted the ensuing free kick off the crossbar and into the net. The Gators held on to the lead through the game to win 1–0 and secure their first national title.

With Fotopoulos gone, Wambach took over as Florida's star player in 1999. That year, she set a school record with 16 assists. She also scored at least 23 goals in each of her last

RECORD SCORER

Danielle Fotopoulos started her collegiate career at Southern Methodist University in 1994. In two seasons with the Mustangs, she scored 52 goals. She added 66 more during her two years at Florida. In 92 college games, Fotopoulos scored 118 goals and tallied 284 points. In 2025, both marks still stood as NCAA records.

Forward Savannah Jordan earned All-America honors all four years at Florida from 2013 to 2016.

three seasons. As a senior in 2001, Wambach helped the Gators win the SEC Tournament for the sixth straight year. And she led them to the semifinals of the NCAA Tournament. However, Santa Clara ended their run there.

Florida missed the NCAA Tournament in 2002. Burleigh then led the Gators to 15 straight tournament appearances. That included three more trips to the Elite Eight. In 2019, Burleigh became the first female coach to win 500 games in Division I soccer. She retired in 2021. In 26 seasons, she led the Gators to 22 NCAA Tournament appearances and 12 SEC Tournament titles.

FACT BOX

First Season: 1995

Location: Gainesville, Florida

Stadium: Donald R. Dizney Stadium

Conference: Southeastern Conference

All-Time Record: 447–176–57

NCAA Tournament Appearances: 22

College Cup Appearances: 2

National Titles: 1998

Top Coaches: Becky Burleigh (1995–2021)

Top Players: Melissa Pini (1995–98); Danielle Fotopoulos (1996–98); Sarah Yohe (1996–99); Andi Sellers (1997–2001); Abby Wambach (1998–2001); Erika Tymrak (2009–12); Christen Westphal (2012–15); Savannah Jordan (2013–16)

Mascot: Albert and Alberta Gator

FLORIDA STATE SEMINOLES

Florida State forward Mami Yamaguchi, *right*, celebrates after scoring against Notre Dame in the 2007 College Cup semifinals.

Florida State established its women's program in 1995. The Seminoles posted a winning record just once over their first five seasons. Since 2000, however, they have consistently been one of the country's best teams.

The team's early NCAA Tournament success came under coach Patrick Baker. That included the Seminoles' first trip to the College Cup in 2003. However, Florida State's transformation into a national power truly began when Mark Krikorian took over in 2005.

Under Krikorian, the team began regularly developing star players.

That included 31 All-Americans and two MAC Hermann Trophy winners. And more importantly, the Seminoles won. Krikorian coached 17 seasons. The team advanced to the second round of the NCAA Tournament each time. Often, it went much farther.

Florida State reached the College Cup in Krikorian's first season. Two years later, it got all the way to the 2007 NCAA title game. The Seminoles finished as national runners-up that year and in 2013 before breaking through in 2014. Senior midfielder Jamia Fields continued her tear through the postseason by scoring in the 1–0 win over Virginia to clinch the title.

Florida State midfielder Jaelin Howell brings the ball up the field against BYU during the 2021 College Cup final.

Beata Olsson and the Seminoles outscored their opponents 21–1 during the 2023 NCAA Tournament.

The postseason success continued with another championship in 2018. This time Dallas Dorosy netted the game-winner as Florida State beat North Carolina 1–0. The senior midfielder was named the College Cup's Most Outstanding Offensive Player. Fellow midfielder Jaelin Howell, a freshman, was the Most Outstanding Defensive Player. That began a dominant stretch for Howell. In 2021, she became only the sixth player to win back-to-back Hermann Trophies. The Seminoles also won a third national title that year. This time they beat BYU 4–3 in a shootout.

Krikorian surprised many by stepping down after that. However, the Seminoles continued to thrive under new coach Brian Pensky. In 2023, they capped the program's first undefeated season with a fourth national title. The final was a battle between the nation's No. 1 and No. 2 teams. Florida State dominated Stanford 5–1. One year later, the Seminoles returned to their 25th NCAA Tournament in a row.

FROM THE WORLD TO TALLAHASSEE

One way Mark Krikorian built up Florida State was by recruiting internationally. In 2007, Japanese forward Mami Yamaguchi became the team's first MAC Hermann Trophy winner. Several other foreign stars followed. The tradition continued after Krikorian left. In 2023, Onyi Echegini, a forward from Nigeria, became the Seminoles' third Hermann Trophy winner.

FACT BOX

First Season: 1995

Location: Tallahassee, Florida

Stadium: Seminole Soccer Complex

Conference: Atlantic Coast Conference

All-Time Record: 476–163–58

NCAA Tournament Appearances: 25

College Cup Appearances: 14

National Titles: 2014, 2018, 2021, 2023

Top Coaches: Patrick Baker (1999–2004); Mark Krikorian (2005–21); Brian Pensky (2022–)

Top Players: Mami Yamaguchi (2005–07); Becky Edwards (2006–09); Tiffany McCarty (2008–09, 2011–12); Dagny Brynjarsdottir (2011–14); Malia Berkely (2016, 2018–20); Jaelin Howell (2018–21); Jenna Nighswonger (2019–22); Onyi Echegini (2022–23)

Mascot: None

NORTH CAROLINA TAR HEELS

Anson Dorrance, *center*, started the North Carolina women's program in 1979 and coached the team for 45 years.

Few teams have dominated any college sport the way North Carolina has in women's soccer. The Tar Heels completed their 46th straight winning season in 2024, a streak that started with the program's founding in 1979. During the run, the Tar Heels completed ten seasons without a loss.

From 1979 to 2023, the program was led by legendary coach Anson Dorrance. In 1981, Dorrance led the team to its first AIAW title. The NCAA took over women's soccer the next season. North Carolina repeated as champions, kicking off a streak of 12 titles in 13 years.

During that stretch, Dorrance coached numerous players who would go on to star for the USWNT. When the United States won the first Women's World Cup in 1991, nine of the team's players were current or former Tar Heels, and Dorrance served as head coach. Several of those stars, including Mia Hamm, Carla Overbeck, and

Forward Mia Hamm scored 103 goals and recorded 72 assists from 1989 to 1993. Both remained North Carolina records in 2025.

Kristine Lilly, led the USWNT to victory again in 1999 on American soil.

North Carolina remained a top team in the 2000s, but as the sport grew, other programs began to catch up. The Tar Heels' streak of 22 straight College Cup appearances ended in 2004. But the team rebounded to win three championships in four years from 2006 to 2009.

Dorrance won his final title with an underdog run in 2012. After an injury-riddled season for the team, North Carolina regrouped in the NCAA Tournament. Led by Crystal Dunn, the Tar Heels knocked out tournament favorites BYU, Stanford, and Penn State to win the championship.

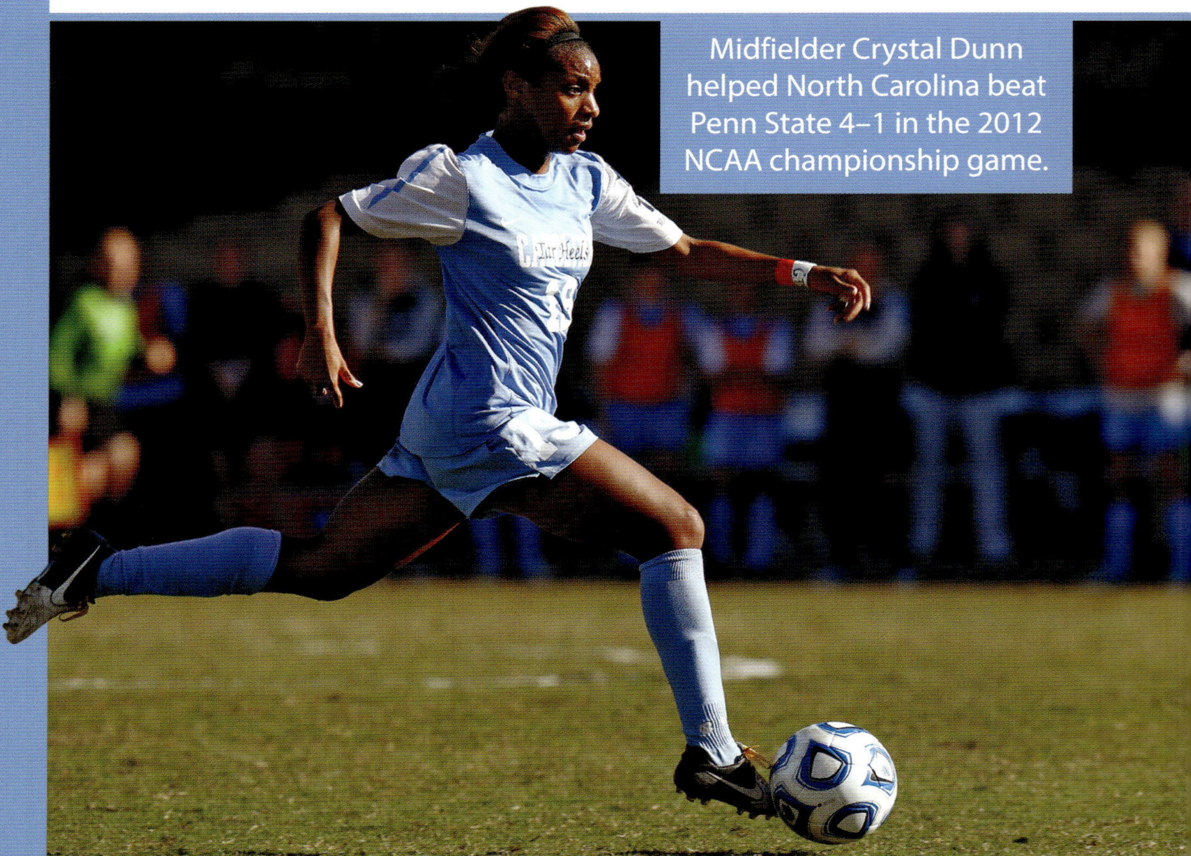

Midfielder Crystal Dunn helped North Carolina beat Penn State 4–1 in the 2012 NCAA championship game.

Dorrance suddenly retired just four days before the 2024 season. His final record was 934–88–53. Assistant Damon Nahas took over and guided the Tar Heels to their first title in 12 years. Including the team's lone AIAW title, it was North Carolina's record-extending 23rd championship.

THE GREATEST EVER?

North Carolina's 2003 team is considered perhaps the greatest ever in college women's soccer. The Tar Heels finished 27–0–0. Led by offensive stars Lindsay Tarpley, Alyssa Ramsey, and Heather O'Reilly, North Carolina outscored its opponents 113–11. O'Reilly netted eight goals in the NCAA Tournament alone. North Carolina blew away its six NCAA Tournament opponents, scoring 32 goals and allowing none.

FACT BOX

First Season: 1979

Location: Chapel Hill, North Carolina

Stadium: Dorrance Field

Conference: Atlantic Coast Conference

All-Time Record: 956–93–53

NCAA Tournament Appearances: 42

College Cup Appearances: 31

National Titles: 1981,* 1982, 1983, 1984, 1986, 1987, 1988, 1989, 1990, 1991, 1992, 1993, 1994, 1996, 1997, 1999, 2000, 2003, 2006, 2008, 2009, 2012, 2024

Top Coaches: Anson Dorrance (1979–2023); Damon Nahas (2024–)

Top Players: April Heinrichs (1983–86); Carla (Werden) Overbeck (1986–89); Kristine Lilly (1989–92); Mia Hamm (1989–90, 1992–93); Tisha Venturini (1991–94); Cindy Parlow (1995–98); Catherine Reddick (2000–03); Crystal Dunn (2010–13)

Mascot: Rameses

*AIAW

23 IN 2024

- North Carolina won its 23rd NCAA championship in women's soccer in December 2024. At the time, no other women's soccer program had more than four.

- The Tar Heels finished 22–5–0 under interim head coach Damon Nahas. He became the second women's college soccer coach to win an NCAA title in his first season.

- North Carolina outscored its opponents 18–1 in six NCAA Tournament games.

Sophomore forward Olivia Thomas was named the 2024 College Cup Most Outstanding Offensive Player after scoring the championship game's only goal.

North Carolina players celebrate after winning the 2024 national championship.

NOTRE DAME FIGHTING IRISH

Teammates rush to celebrate with goalkeeper Erika Bohn after Notre Dame won the 2004 national title.

Two years after starting its women's soccer program, Notre Dame hired Chris Petrucelli as coach in 1990. Under Petrucelli, the Fighting Irish reached their first NCAA Tournament in 1993. The next year, they entered the tournament with an undefeated record. Notre Dame made it all the way to the championship game before losing to North Carolina.

Those two teams met again in the semifinals of the 1995 NCAA Tournament. In the 20th minute, the Irish scored when a header from Cindy Daws was accidentally directed into the goal by a North Carolina player for an own goal. That proved to be enough, as Notre Dame won 1–0. The victory ended North Carolina's streak of nine consecutive national titles.

Daws then proved to be the hero in the title game, too. Notre Dame and Portland went deep into extra time with neither team having scored. Finally, with time running out, Notre Dame earned a free kick from just outside the penalty area. Daws quickly knocked it in, giving the Irish their first national title.

Petrucelli left Notre Dame after the 1998 season. New coach Randy Waldrum got off to a fast start. The Irish reached the NCAA title game in his first season but lost to North Carolina.

Notre Dame made it back to the national title game in 2004. With the game tied 1–1 late, UCLA earned a penalty kick. Notre Dame keeper Erika Bohn made a diving save to keep

In 2008, Notre Dame forward Kerri Hanks, *left*, became the only Division I women's soccer player to record at least 73 goals and 73 assists in her career.

Notre Dame coach Randy Waldrum, *right*, lifts the NCAA championship trophy in 2010.

her team's title hopes alive. The game eventually came down to a shootout. Bohn turned away another penalty shot there to secure Notre Dame's second national title.

In 2005, Kerri Hanks arrived at Notre Dame. The star forward went on to earn All-America honors all four years with the Irish. As a senior in 2008, she became only the fourth player to win the MAC Hermann Trophy twice. Hanks also led Notre Dame to runner-up finishes in the NCAA Tournament in 2006 and 2008.

In 2010, the Fighting Irish returned to the championship game. Facing an undefeated Stanford team, Waldrum was confident Notre Dame would win. He told freshman forward Adriana Leon before the game that she would score. That's exactly what happened.

Leon scored in the 63rd minute. Her goal lifted the Fighting Irish to a 1–0 win and their third national title. In 2022, the Irish got back to the Elite Eight for the first time in ten years.

BRICK WALL

During the 1995 NCAA Tournament, no one could score on Jen Renola. The goalkeeper recorded six shutouts to help the Fighting Irish win their first national title. That momentum carried over into 1996 for Renola. That season, the National Soccer Coaches Association of America named her the National Player of the Year.

FACT BOX

First Season: 1988

Location: Notre Dame, Indiana

Stadium: Alumni Stadium

Conference: Atlantic Coast Conference

All-Time Record: 625–159–56

NCAA Tournament Appearances: 30

College Cup Appearances: 12

National Titles: 1995, 2004, 2010

Top Coaches: Chris Petrucelli (1990–98); Randy Waldrum (1999–2013)

Top Players: Cindy Daws (1993–96); Jen Renola (1993–96); Monica Gerardo (1995–98); Jenny Streiffer (1996–99); Anne Makinen (1997–2000); Katie Thorlakson (2002–05); Kerri Hanks (2005–08); Melissa Henderson (2008–11)

Mascot: The Leprechaun

PENN STATE NITTANY LIONS

Penn State forward Christie Welsh poses with the MAC Hermann Trophy in 2001.

Pennsylvania State, better known as Penn State, first reached the NCAA Tournament in 1995. That was only the Nittany Lions' second season. Three years later, they won their first Big Ten Tournament title.

Forward Christie Welsh led the team to new heights. As a freshman in 1999, she set school records with 27 goals and 13 assists. The Nittany Lions also reached the College Cup semifinals for the first time. In 2001, under new coach Paula Wilkins, Welsh became the school's all-time leader in goals and assists on the way to winning the MAC Hermann Trophy. Then, as a senior in 2002, she led Penn State back to the College Cup semifinals.

Welsh and Tiffany Weimer made for a strong forward line during that 2002 season. Weimer continued to take off after

Welsh left. She scored 32 goals in 2005, breaking Welsh's school record. She also led Penn State into the NCAA Tournament with an undefeated record. The Nittany Lions made it to the semifinals before losing to Portland in a shootout.

Wilkins left Penn State after the 2006 season. Under coach Erica Dambach, the Nittany Lions won their 15th straight Big Ten regular-season title in 2012. They then made another run to the NCAA Tournament semifinals. Christine Nairn scored

Nittany Lions forward Maya Hayes was a first team All-American in 2011 and 2012.

Penn State's Rocky Rodriguez, *right*, races past a Duke defender during the 2015 College Cup final.

a quick extra time goal against Florida State to send Penn State to its first national championship game. However, North Carolina beat Penn State 4–1.

The Nittany Lions got back to the title game in 2015. Raquel "Rocky" Rodriguez was a big reason why. The attacking midfielder and MAC Hermann Trophy winner continued to shine against Duke in the NCAA title game. She scored the go-ahead goal in the 72nd minute. Some key saves by goalkeeper Britt Eckerstrom secured her eighth straight shutout and a 1–0 win, giving the Nittany Lions their first national title.

Dambach continued to lead Penn State to successful seasons. In 2022, the team won its ninth Big Ten Tournament title. In 2024, the Nittany Lions played in their 30th straight NCAA Tournament.

NEW POSITION, SAME RESULT

In 2005, Ali Krieger earned first-team All-America honors as a midfielder. Before her senior year in 2006, she moved back and played as a defender. Krieger thrived in her new position and was a first team All-American again. She's the only Penn State player to be an All-American in two different positions.

FACT BOX

First Season: 1994

Location: University Park, Pennsylvania

Stadium: Jeffrey Field

Conference: Big Ten Conference

All-Time Record: 531–152–51

NCAA Tournament Appearances: 30

College Cup Appearances: 5

National Titles: 2015

Top Coaches: Paula Wilkins (2001–07); Erica Dambach (2007–)

Top Players: Emily Oleksiuk (1998–2001); Christie Welsh (1999–2002); Tiffany Weimer (2002–05); Ali Krieger (2003–06); Alyssa Naeher (2006–09); Maya Hayes (2010–13); Rocky Rodriguez (2012–15); Ally Schlegel (2019–22)

Mascot: The Nittany Lion

PORTLAND PILOTS

In 2005, Portland became the third women's soccer program to win multiple NCAA championships, joining North Carolina and Notre Dame.

Portland first fielded a women's soccer team in 1980. Six years later, the Pilots started competing in Division I. That season, Portland began a streak of 24 straight winning records.

The program truly took off in the 1990s under coach Clive Charles. Portland reached its first NCAA Tournament in 1992 and its first College Cup semifinal in 1994. Led by stars Shannon MacMillan and Tiffeny Milbrett, the Pilots were undefeated in the regular season in 1995 and reached the College Cup final. There, they fell 1–0 on an extra time goal against Notre Dame.

Charles led Portland back to the College Cup in 1996, 1998, 2000, and 2001. Each time, the Pilots fell in the semifinals. All four losses came by one goal.

Portland entered the 2002 tournament as the No. 8 seed. The Pilots didn't allow a goal in their first five games but still faced a close call in the Elite Eight. Following a scoreless draw, Portland outlasted Stanford in a shootout to reach the College Cup again. This time the Pilots beat Penn State 2–0 to reach the championship against fierce conference rival Santa Clara.

The Broncos were defending national champions and had defeated Portland 1–0 during the regular season. Portland fell behind in the first half. But the team leaned on scoring star Christine Sinclair. The Canadian

Portland teammates Megan Rapinoe (3) and Christine Sinclair both went on to historic careers with their national teams.

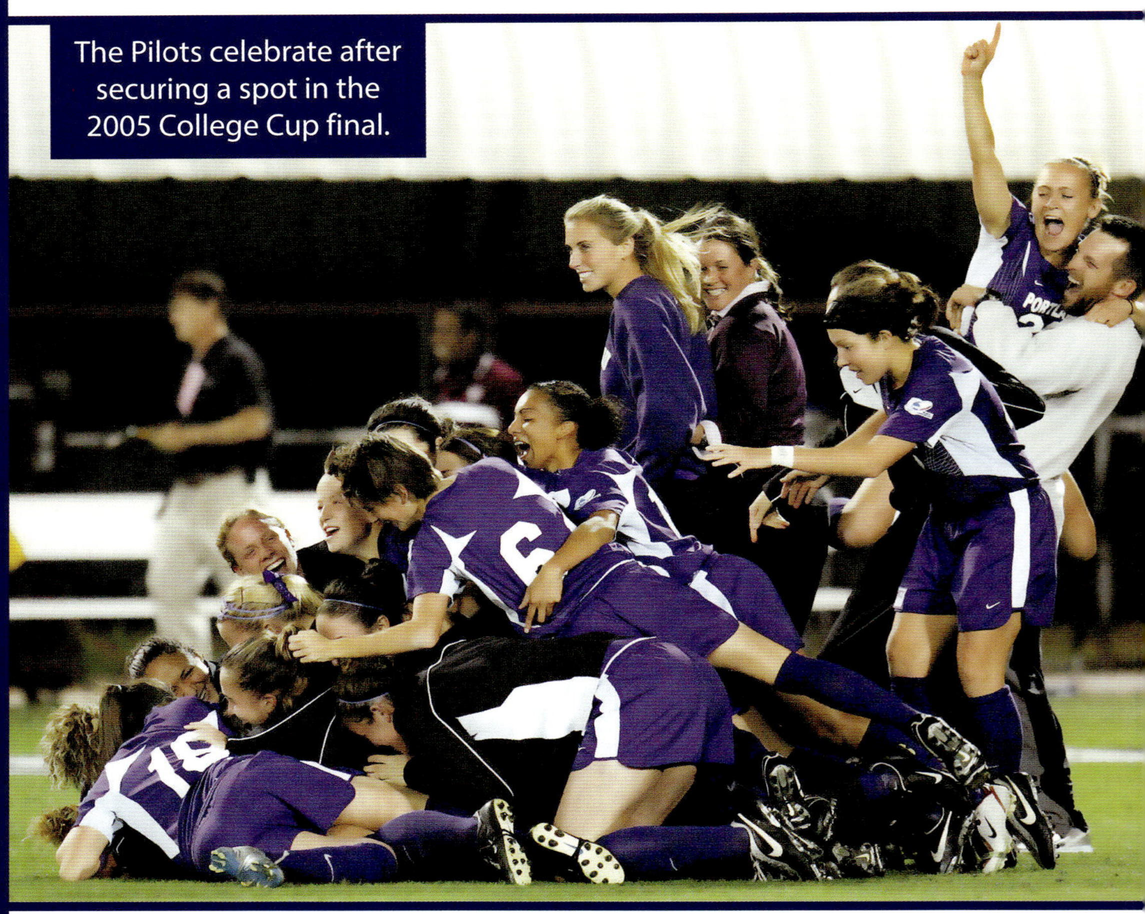

The Pilots celebrate after securing a spot in the 2005 College Cup final.

forward scored in the 61st minute to tie the game. She then scored on a rebound in the second extra time to clinch Portland's first national championship.

Charles, who was battling cancer, left the team after the 2002 title. He died a year later. In 2005, Sinclair teamed up with future USWNT star Megan Rapinoe to deliver a second championship. Sinclair scored twice while Rapinoe added a goal and an assist in the title game. Portland routed UCLA 4–0.

Afterward, coach Garrett Smith dedicated the championship to Charles. However, Portland eventually fell off. From 2014 to 2024, the Pilots made just one NCAA Tournament.

SCORING MACHINE

In 2002, Christine Sinclair finished the NCAA Tournament with a record ten goals. That was one of many records the Canadian forward smashed in her career. Sinclair scored a season-record 39 times in 2005. She also joined the Canadian national team during her college career. Sinclair retired from international play in 2023 with an all-time record 190 international goals.

FACT BOX

First Season: 1980

Location: Portland, Oregon

Stadium: Merlo Field

Conference: West Coast Conference

All-Time Record: 587–231–78

NCAA Tournament Appearances: 22

College Cup Appearances: 8

National Titles: 2002, 2005

Top Coaches: Clive Charles (1989–2002); Garrett Smith (2003–17)

Top Players: Tiffeny Milbrett (1990–92, 1994); Shannon MacMillan (1992–95); Justi Baumgardt (1993, 1995–97); Michelle French (1995–98); Lauren Orlandos (1999–2002); Christine Sinclair (2001–02, 2004–05); Megan Rapinoe (2005–08); Danielle Foxhoven (2008–11)

Mascot: Wally Pilot

RUTGERS SCARLET KNIGHTS

Rutgers began its women's soccer program in 1984. The Scarlet Knights reached their first NCAA Tournament three years later. However, Rutgers lost its tournament opener 1–0 to UConn.

The Scarlet Knights didn't return to the tournament until 2001. Freshman star and future USWNT standout Carli Lloyd scored 15 goals that season. In the NCAA Tournament, Rutgers beat Boston University 4–1 and in-state rival Princeton 1–0. Eventual champion North Carolina finally stopped the Scarlet Knights with a 2–1 win in the third round.

Carli Lloyd scored a school-record 50 goals for Rutgers from 2001 to 2004.

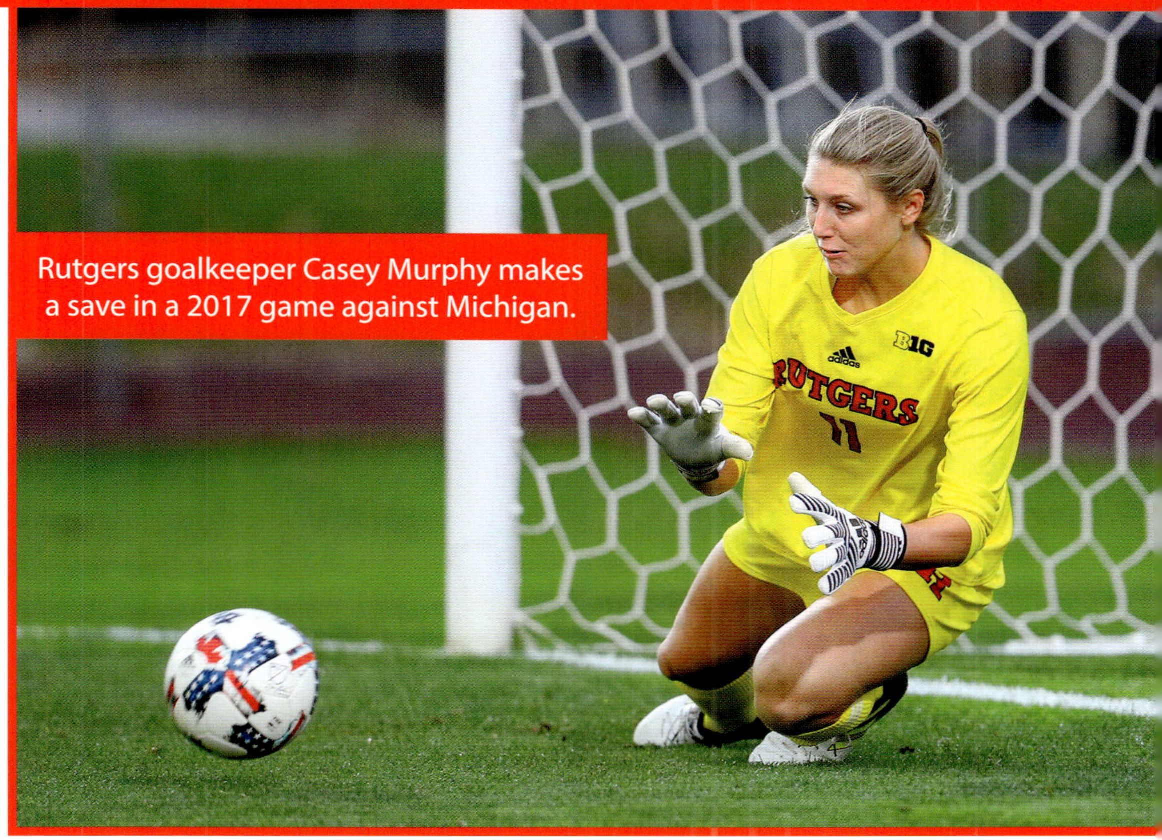

Rutgers goalkeeper Casey Murphy makes a save in a 2017 game against Michigan.

That season was the start of a record-setting career for Lloyd. She led the team to another NCAA Tournament appearance in 2003. Lloyd left the program in 2005 as the Scarlet Knights' all-time leader with 50 goals and 117 points.

Coach Glenn Crooks led Rutgers to the NCAA Tournament seven times in 14 seasons. The Scarlet Knights took the next step in 2015 under second-year coach Mike O'Neill. In the NCAA Tournament, Rutgers and No. 1 Virginia played to a 0–0 draw in the Elite Eight. Goalkeeper Casey Murphy had already enjoyed a record-setting season. Her decisive save in the shootout clinched the Scarlet Knights' first trip to the College Cup. However, Penn State beat Rutgers in the semifinals.

Rutgers entered the 2021 NCAA Tournament as a No. 1 seed. In the Elite Eight, the team outlasted Arkansas in a shootout

Rutgers forward Amirah Ali was a MAC Hermann Trophy semifinalist in 2021 after scoring 12 goals.

to reach another College Cup. The Scarlet Knights then fell behind Florida State 1–0 in the semifinals. Despite several chances late in the game, Rutgers was unable to tie it up. But under O'Neill, the Scarlet Knights continued to have success. The team reached its 13th straight NCAA Tournament in 2024.

SHUTTING IT DOWN

Rutgers goalkeeper Casey Murphy tied the NCAA record with 19 shutouts in 2015. Over 67 games between 2014 and 2017, she recorded 45 shutouts. That put her ninth on the NCAA's all-time list. The goalies ahead of her all appeared in at least eight more games.

FACT BOX

First Season: 1984

Location: New Brunswick, New Jersey

Stadium: Yurcak Field

Conference: Big Ten Conference

All-Time Record: 469–266–102

NCAA Tournament Appearances: 18

College Cup Appearances: 2

National Titles: None

Top Coaches: Glenn Crooks (2000–13); Mike O'Neill (2014–)

Top Players: Robin Copperthwaite (1984–87); Kris Kurzynowski (1988–91); Saskia Webber (1989–92); Carli Lloyd (2001–04); Jonelle Filigno (2010–13); Casey Murphy (2014–17); Amirah Ali (2017–21); Gabby Provenzano (2017–21)

Mascot: Sir Henry

SANTA CLARA BRONCOS

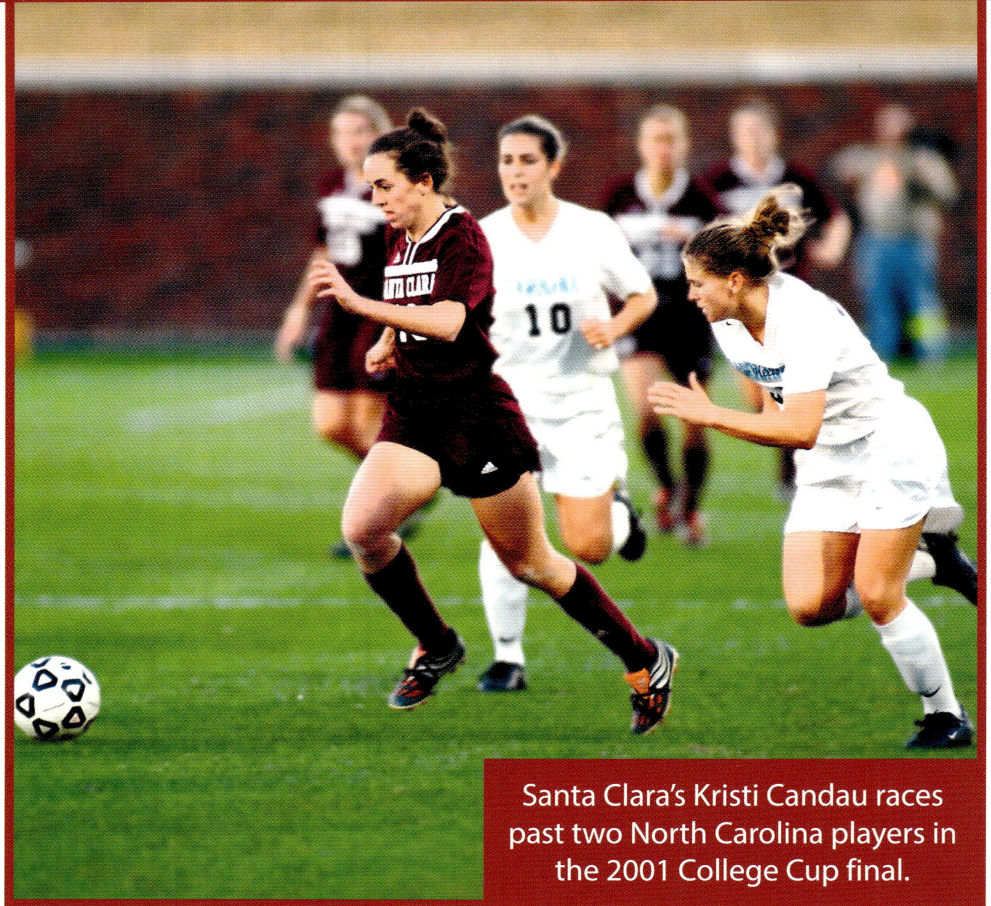

Santa Clara's Kristi Candau races past two North Carolina players in the 2001 College Cup final.

Santa Clara finished its first season in 1980 with a 1–6–1 record. But it didn't take long for the Broncos to begin an excellent winning run. Starting in 1984, Santa Clara didn't suffer another losing season until 2008.

Most of that success has come under longtime coach Jerry Smith. He was in only his third season when he guided Santa Clara to its first NCAA Tournament in 1989. Behind future USWNT star Brandi Chastain, the Broncos reached back-to-back

College Cups in 1989 and 1990. By 1999, the team had reached the College Cup seven times. However, each time, the Broncos lost in the semifinal round.

Santa Clara finally broke through in 2001 behind the play of star forward Aly Wagner. The Broncos led Florida 2–0 in the semifinal round before the Gators rallied to force extra time. Finally, Santa Clara's Veronica Zepeda scored on a rebound to win the game 3–2.

Midfielder Aly Wagner became the second player in Santa Clara history to win the MAC Hermann Trophy when she took home the award in 2002.

In its first title game, Santa Clara faced a North Carolina team playing in its 19th final in 20 years. Wagner scored on a shot to the upper left corner with only a few minutes remaining in the first half. That proved to be enough as Santa Clara held on for a 1–0 victory and its first championship.

Smith considered leaving Santa Clara to coach Notre Dame in 2014. He ultimately decided to stay with the Broncos. In 2021, he became the third women's coach to reach 500 wins, joining North Carolina's Anson Dorrance and UConn's Len Tsantiris.

That year, Santa Clara reached the College Cup final against Florida State. After trailing 1–0 for much of the game, Santa Clara's Kelsey Turnbow made a weaving run and scored on a

Santa Clara's Kelsey Turnbow celebrates after scoring the tying goal in the 2020 College Cup final against Florida State.

well-placed low shot to tie the score in the 84th minute. The game eventually went to a shootout. Florida State hit the post twice, and Santa Clara's Izzy D'Aquila converted the clinching score to deliver the Broncos' second national championship.

SHUTTING IT DOWN

The Broncos set an NCAA record with 16 consecutive shutouts in 1998. The streak began with a 1–0 win over California on September 24. It ended in a 1–0 loss to Florida in the College Cup semifinals on December 4. In total, Santa Clara allowed only four total goals during the 1998 season.

FACT BOX

First Season: 1980

Location: Santa Clara, California

Stadium: Stevens Stadium

Conference: West Coast Conference

All-Time Record: 628–216–91

NCAA Tournament Appearances: 34

College Cup Appearances: 12

National Titles: 2001, 2020

Top Coaches: Phil Wright (1981–84); Jerry Smith (1987–)

Top Players: Jenni Symons (1985–88); Brandi Chastain (1989–90); Deb Norbutas (1989–92); Jennifer Lalor (1992–94, 1996); Mandy Clemens (1996–99); Aly Wagner (1998–2002); Julie Johnston (2010–13); Kelsey Turnbow (2017–21)

Mascot: Bucky the Bronco

STANFORD CARDINAL

Stanford qualified for its twelfth College Cup in 2024.

Stanford founded its women's soccer program in 1984. After four losing seasons, the Cardinal won 13 games in 1988 under second-year coach Berhane Anderberhan. Through 2024, Stanford still hadn't had another losing season.

Led by star freshman midfielder Julie Foudy, the Cardinal reached the NCAA Tournament for the first time in 1990. Stanford returned to the tournament every season in the 1990s except for one. That stretch included the school's first College Cup semifinal appearance in 1993.

Coach Paul Ratcliffe took over in 2003. By 2009, he had turned the Cardinal into a premier soccer program. That season, Stanford reached the first of three straight College Cup finals. The Cardinal lost the first two. But in 2011, the Cardinal broke through with a 1–0 championship-game victory over Duke. MAC Hermann Trophy winner Teresa Noyola headed in the winning goal early in the second half to cap a 25–0–1 season.

Cardinal forward Christen Press won the MAC Hermann Trophy in 2010.

Noyola was one of a long line of Hermann Trophy winners to play for Ratcliffe. Between 2009 and 2019, Stanford produced six Hermann Trophy winners. Kelley O'Hara, Christen Press, and Noyola won three straight from 2009 to 2011. Andi Sullivan won the award in 2017. The midfielder helped Stanford get back to the College Cup final that year. Then she scored to help Stanford build a 2–0 halftime lead over rival UCLA. The Bruins tied the game in the second half. But in the 67th minute, Jaye Boissiere's long-range shot clinched Stanford's second national title.

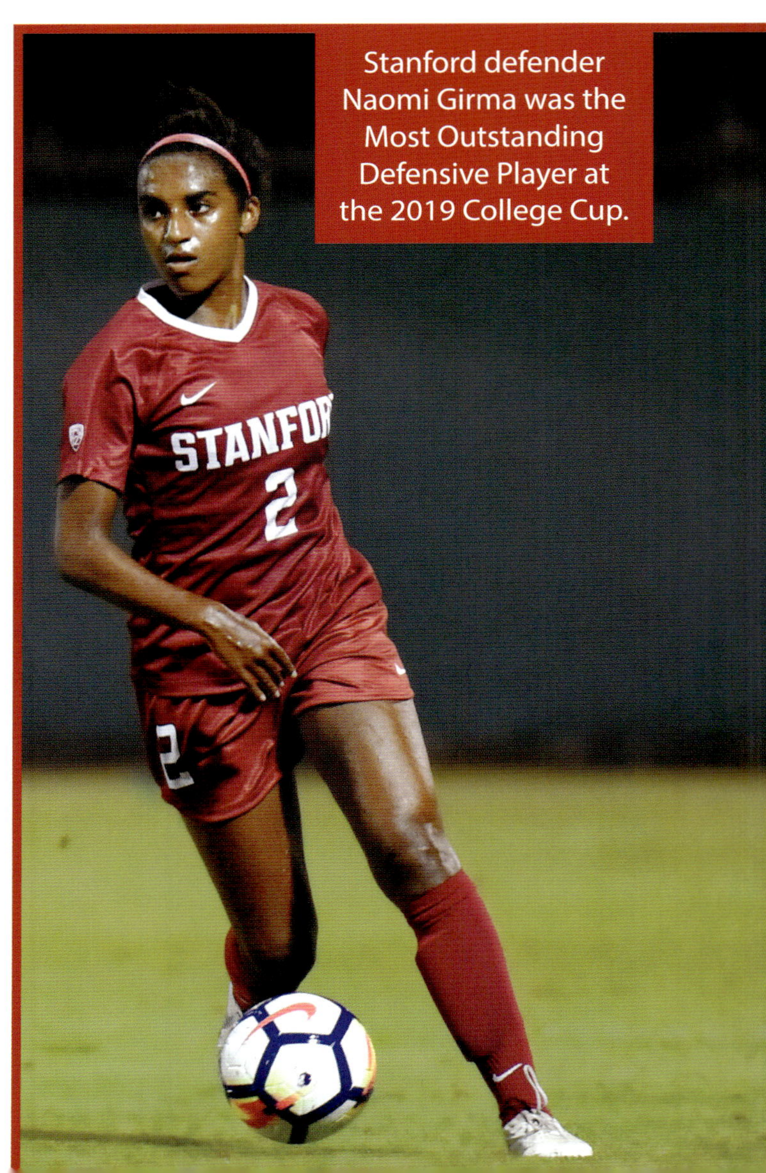

Stanford defender Naomi Girma was the Most Outstanding Defensive Player at the 2019 College Cup.

Two years later, the Cardinal were led by two-time Hermann Trophy winner Catarina Macario and defender Naomi Girma. The future USWNT stars led a 23–1–0 team into the College Cup final against North Carolina. Neither team could score in regulation or extra time. In a shootout to decide the national title, Cardinal freshman goalkeeper Katie Meyer made two saves. Junior midfielder Kiki Pickett sealed the win in the sixth round by beating the goalkeeper with a low shot just inside the post.

A CLEAN SWEEP

Stanford's 2017 College Cup victory over UCLA set up a college soccer first. One week later, the Cardinal men's team beat Indiana 1–0 for their third title. In doing so, Stanford became the first school to win both the men's and women's soccer championships in the same season.

FACT BOX

First Season: 1984

Location: Palo Alto, California

Stadium: Laird Q. Cagan Stadium

Conference: Atlantic Coast Conference

All-Time Record: 583–168–61

NCAA Tournament Appearances: 33

College Cup Appearances: 12

National Titles: 2011, 2017, 2019

Top Coaches: Berhane Anderberhan (1987–92); Paul Ratcliffe (2003–)

Top Players: Julie Foudy (1989–92); Sarah Rafanelli (1990–93); Kelley O'Hara (2006–09); Christen Press (2007–10); Teresa Noyola (2008–11); Andi Sullivan (2014–17); Catarina Macario (2017–19); Naomi Girma (2018–21)

Mascot: The Tree (unofficial)

TEXAS A&M AGGIES

Texas A&M didn't start its women's soccer program until 1993. But the Aggies were immediately successful. Under coach G Guerrieri, Texas A&M won 15 games in each of its first two seasons. Then, in 1995, the team went 17–5 to reach its first NCAA Tournament. While many outsiders didn't consider the Aggies a nationally competitive team, Texas A&M proved itself by winning its first NCAA Tournament game 4–1 over Clemson.

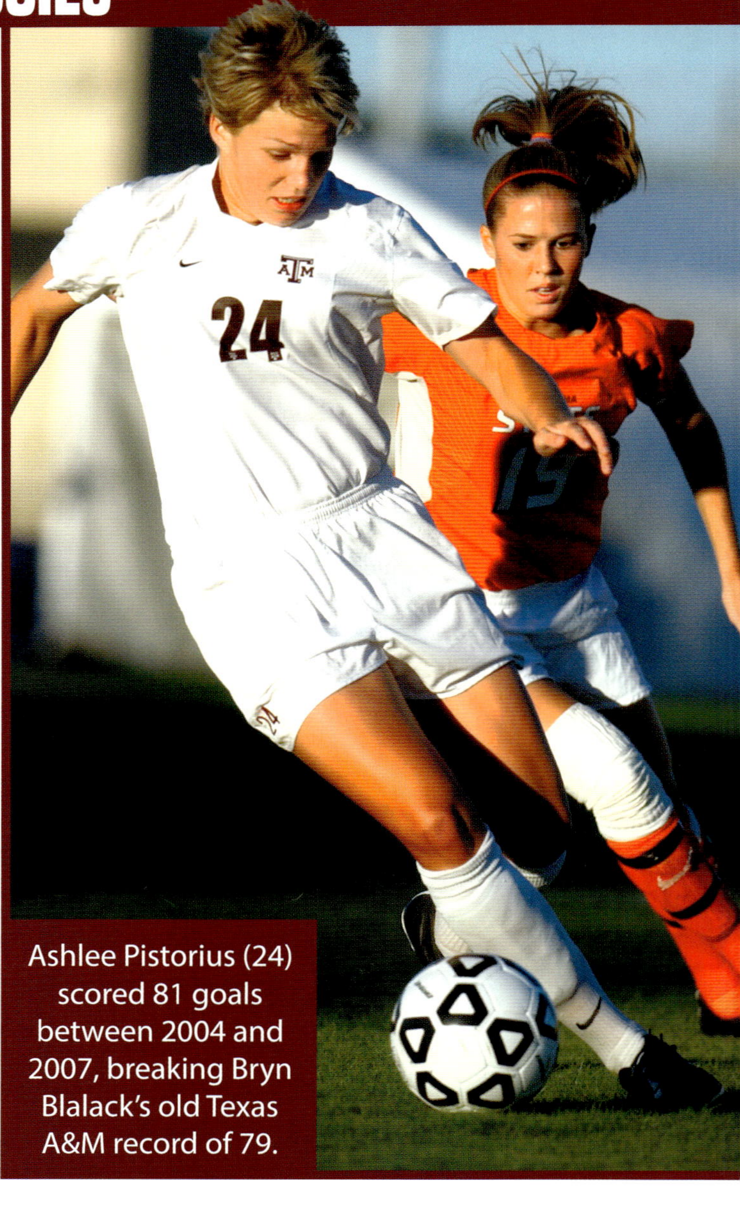

Ashlee Pistorius (24) scored 81 goals between 2004 and 2007, breaking Bryn Blalack's old Texas A&M record of 79.

The Aggies moved into the brand-new Big 12 Conference when it began play in 1996. Led by record-setting forward Bryn Blalack, Texas A&M went 8–1 in conference play and returned to the NCAA Tournament. The Aggies won their first Big 12 title in 1997. They added six more before leaving the conference for the SEC in 2012.

Texas A&M opened its SEC era by reaching its eighteenth NCAA Tournament in a row. Two years later, in 2014, the Aggies made their deepest run yet. Entering the field as one of four No. 1 seeds, they beat Houston Baptist and Arizona by a combined 12–2 margin in the first two rounds. The Aggies then knocked off traditional power Notre Dame 2–1 in the third round. In the Elite Eight, Texas A&M topped Penn State 2–1 on two goals from Allie Bailey. With the win, the Aggies qualified for the College Cup for the first time.

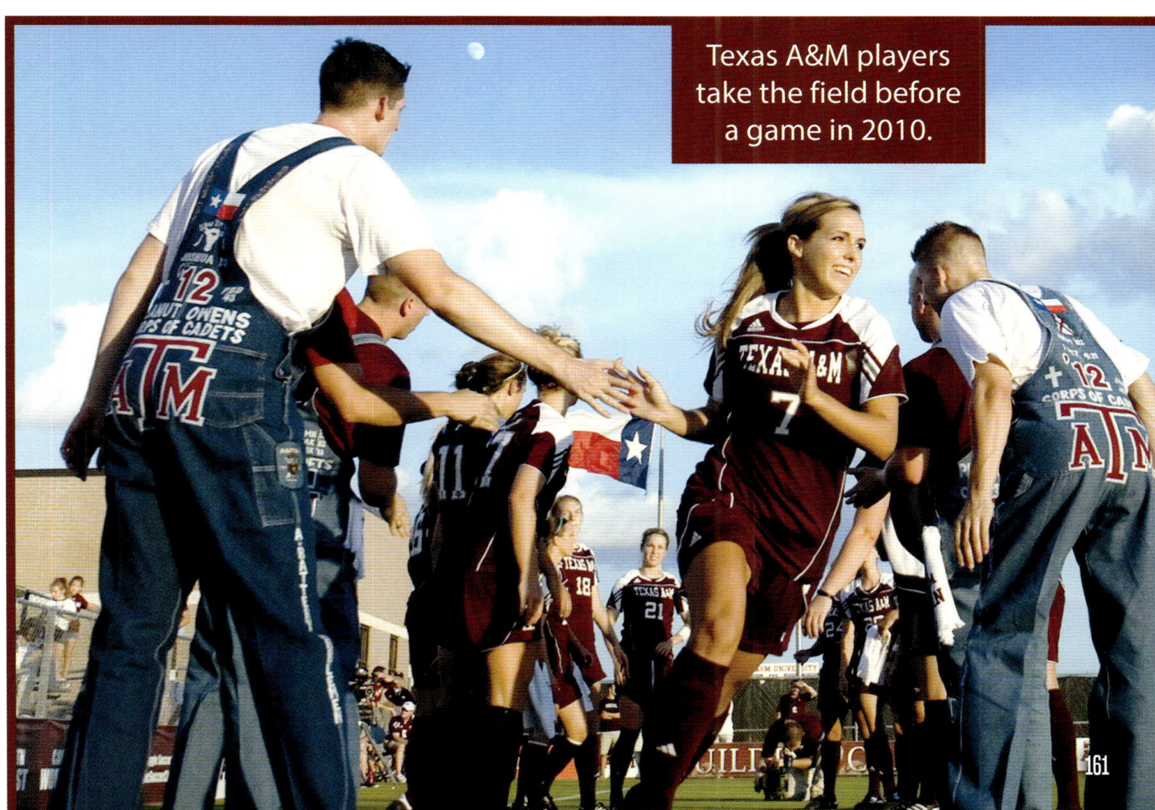

Texas A&M players take the field before a game in 2010.

The Aggies' Allie Bailey, *right*, celebrates her go-ahead goal against Penn State in the 2014 Elite Eight.

HOME FIELD ADVANTAGE

Texas A&M has long attracted big crowds to Ellis Field. From 2002 to 2022, the Aggies ranked third in the nation in overall attendance. Texas A&M led the country in attendance six times during that stretch. The NCAA took notice as well. Ellis Field hosted the College Cup in 2005, 2007, and 2009.

Texas A&M faced Virginia in the semifinals. The Aggies fell behind early. Kelley Monogue scored her 18th goal of the season 32 minutes in to tie it up 1–1. But the Cavaliers scored just before halftime and added a third goal in the second half to win 3–1.

Texas A&M's streak of 26 straight NCAA Tournament appearances ended in 2021. That year, the team finished with a losing record for the first time in program history. The Aggies bounced back quickly. They reached the NCAA Tournament in each of the next two seasons.

FACT BOX

First Season: 1993

Location: College Station, Texas

Stadium: Ellis Field

Conference: Southeastern Conference

All-Time Record: 502–173–53

NCAA Tournament Appearances: 28

College Cup Appearances: 1

National Titles: None

Top Coaches: G Guerrieri (1993–)

Top Players: Bryn Blalack (1994–97); Melanie Wilson (1996–2000); Kati Jo Spisak (2002–05); Ashlee Pistorius (2004–07); Amy Berend (2004–07); Melissa Garey (2004–07); Bri Young (2008–11); Ally Watt (2015–19)

Mascot: Reveille

UCLA BRUINS

Joy Fawcett was still in the prime of her USWNT career when the University of California, Los Angeles (UCLA) hired her as its first coach in 1993. Her Bruins got off to a strong start. She led the program to five straight winning seasons. UCLA also reached its first NCAA Tournament in 1995 under Fawcett. Two years later, the Bruins recorded their first NCAA Tournament win with a 1–0 victory over traditional power Portland.

Fawcett surprised many by stepping down after the 1997 season. She wanted to focus on her family and USWNT career, which continued until 2004. After one season under Todd Saldana, Jillian Ellis took over in 1999. She nearly led the Bruins to a miraculous national title in her second season. Stephanie Rigamat scored late as UCLA beat Portland again in the College Cup semifinals. UCLA then held a 1–0 lead late in the title game against North Carolina. But the Tar Heels scored twice in the final 15 minutes to win 2–1.

UCLA's Iris Mora kicks downfield in the 2005 College Cup final against Portland.

UCLA had to wait another 13 years for its championship breakthrough.

UCLA players hold up the NCAA championship trophy after beating Florida State in the 2013 title game.

The 2013 team tied a program record with 22 wins under coach Amanda Cromwell. Led by future USWNT stars Abby Dahlkemper and Sam Mewis, the Bruins reached the championship game against Florida State. After a scoreless regulation, Kodi Lavrusky's goal seven minutes into extra time secured UCLA its first national championship.

Nearly a decade later, the Bruins took part in another thrilling title game. Under first-year coach Margueritte Aozasa,

UCLA reached the 2022 College Cup final, once again against North Carolina. The Tar Heels led 2–0 with just over ten minutes to play. Then UCLA mounted a dramatic comeback. Lexi Wright scored to make it 2–1. Then Reilyn Turner tied the game with 16 seconds left. And seven minutes into extra time, Maricarmen Reyes put UCLA in front 3–2 on a close-range rebound shot. The Bruins held on from there to clinch a dramatic second title.

EARLY SUCCESS

Jillian Ellis took UCLA to the 2000 College Cup final in her second season as coach. Amanda Cromwell had only been UCLA coach for eight months when her Bruins won the 2013 national championship. Cromwell left the position in December 2021. Less than a year later, Marguerite Aozasa became the first rookie head coach to win a women's title.

UCLA's Maricarmen Reyes lines up the go-ahead shot in extra time of the 2022 College Cup final against North Carolina.

FACT BOX

First Season: 1993

Location: Los Angeles, California

Stadium: Wallis Annenberg Stadium

Conference: Big Ten Conference

All-Time Record: 549–115–53

NCAA Tournament Appearances: 28

College Cup Appearances: 12

National Titles: 2013, 2022

Top Coaches: Jillian Ellis (2000–10); Amanda Cromwell (2013–21); Margueritte Aozasa (2022–)

Top Players: Traci Arkenberg (1994–97); Nandi Pryce (2000–03); Lauren Cheney (2006–09); Sydney Leroux (2008–11); Abby Dahlkemper (2011–14); Sam Mewis (2011–14); Jessie Fleming (2016–19); Lilly Reale (2021–24)

Mascot: Joe and Josephine Bruin

USC TROJANS

USC and rival UCLA both founded women's soccer programs in 1993. The teams were rivals in the Pac-10/Pac-12 conference before both moved to the Big Ten in 2024.

The University of Southern California (USC) quickly built a winning program after its founding in 1993. Jim Millinder coached the Trojans from 1996 to 2006. His teams never had a losing record.

Along the way, Millinder's teams reached eight NCAA Tournaments. USC's first appearance came in 1998, led by stars Kim Clark and four-time All-American Isabelle Harvey.

The Trojans also won their first NCAA Tournament game that season, beating conference-rival Washington 2–1 in extra time.

Though consistently good under Millinder, USC didn't reach the third round of the NCAA Tournament until the year after he left. The Trojans entered the 2007 NCAA Tournament with a 14–3–2 record. Then they posted four straight shutouts to reach the College Cup semifinals against archrival UCLA. Both teams were bidding to become the first national champion in women's soccer from the Pac-10 Conference. USC fell behind in the 38th minute before Trojans attacker Amy Rodriguez scored twice late in the game to seal the comeback win.

Teammates rush to celebrate with Janessa Currier (15) after she scored USC's second goal in the 2007 College Cup final.

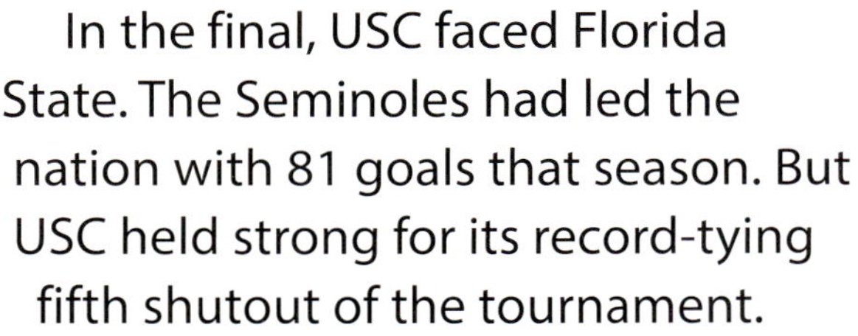

In the final, USC faced Florida State. The Seminoles had led the nation with 81 goals that season. But USC held strong for its record-tying fifth shutout of the tournament. Goals from Marihelen Tomer and Janessa Currier propelled the Trojans to a 2–0 win.

Morgan Andrews holds up the championship trophy after USC's 3–1 win over West Virginia in the 2016 College Cup final.

LEAGUE OF NATIONS

USC players have competed in the Women's World Cup for six different nations. In 1999, Susie Mora suited up for Mexico and Isabelle Harvey played for Canada. Amy Rodriguez was a USWNT player in 2011 and 2015. Olufolasade Adamolekun went to the 2019 tournament for Jamaica. In 2023, Savannah DeMelo played for the United States. Meanwhile, Simi Awujo (Canada), Ashleigh Plumptre (Nigeria), and Dominique Randall (Philippines) also took part.

After three consecutive losing seasons, USC hired Keidane McAlpine to take over as coach in 2014. McAlpine led a quick turnaround. In 2016, the Trojans allowed only 12 goals all season. Five of those goals came in their first four games.

USC entered the NCAA Tournament as a No. 2 seed. Once again, the Trojans' defense came up big. They posted three straight 1–0 shutouts to reach the College Cup final against No. 1 West Virginia. USC forward Morgan Andrews scored less than two minutes into the game. After the Mountaineers tied it in the 66th minute, Trojans senior Katie Johnson tallied twice in a 12-minute span to seal USC's second title.

FACT BOX

First Season: 1993

Location: Los Angeles, California

Stadium: MacAlister Field

Conference: Big Ten Conference

All-Time Record: 396–194–72

NCAA Tournament Appearances: 23

College Cup Appearances: 6

National Titles: 2007, 2016

Top Coaches: Jim Millinder (1996–2006); Ali Khosroshahin (2007–13); Keidane McAlpine (2014–21)

Top Players: Kim Clark (1996–99); Isabelle Harvey (1996–2000); Kristin Olsen (2006–09); Morgan Andrews (2015–16); Ally Prisock (2015–18); Penelope Hocking (2018–21); Croix Bethune (2020–22)

Mascot: Traveler

VIRGINIA CAVALIERS

The Cavaliers won their first ACC regular-season title in 2004, and they added another in 2012.

Virginia founded its women's soccer program in 1985. In their first 40 seasons, the Cavaliers had winning records in all but one year. The exception was 1986, when they finished 8–8–2.

A year later, Virginia reached its first NCAA Tournament. Though the Cavaliers missed the tournament in 1993, they returned a year later. That began a new streak of 30 straight appearances. Actually winning in the tournament proved tougher, though. Between 1994 and 2012, the Cavaliers never advanced past the Elite Eight.

Coach Steve Swanson put together Virginia's breakthrough season in 2013. Led by MAC Hermann Trophy–winning midfielder Morgan Brian, the Cavaliers led the nation with 78 goals. They finished a program-best 24–1–1. Virginia entered the NCAA Tournament ranked No. 1 and outscored its first four opponents 10–1 to reach the College Cup semifinals. Facing UCLA, Makenzy Doniak scored in the second half to put the Cavaliers up 1–0. But the Bruins rallied to tie the game with less than five minutes left. After a scoreless extra time, UCLA advanced in a shootout.

Brian won her second straight Hermann Trophy in 2014 while leading Virginia to a 23–3–0 record. The Cavaliers reached the College Cup again. This time they advanced to the final with a 3–1 victory over Texas A&M. Doniak, Emily Sonnett, and Alexis Shaffer all scored. Virginia had

Morgan Brian made her debut for the USWNT in 2013 after winning her first MAC Hermann Trophy with Virginia.

scored three goals or more 17 times in 25 games entering the final. However, the Cavaliers were shut out 1–0 by Florida State.

Virginia, this time riding a stout defense, reached its fourth College Cup in the 2020 tournament, which was delayed until 2021. The Cavaliers allowed only one goal in five

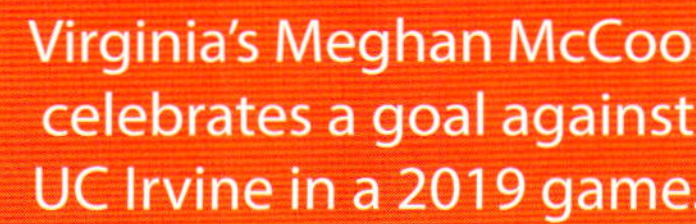

Virginia's Meghan McCool celebrates a goal against UC Irvine in a 2019 game.

NCAA Tournament games. Once again, they faced ACC-rival Florida State, this time in the semifinals. After both teams failed to score in regulation, the Seminoles won in a shootout.

WINNING TRADITION

Virginia finished 13–5–1 during the 2024 season to continue an impressive streak. It was the Cavaliers' 38th straight winning season. Only conference rival North Carolina, at 43 straight years, has had a longer run.

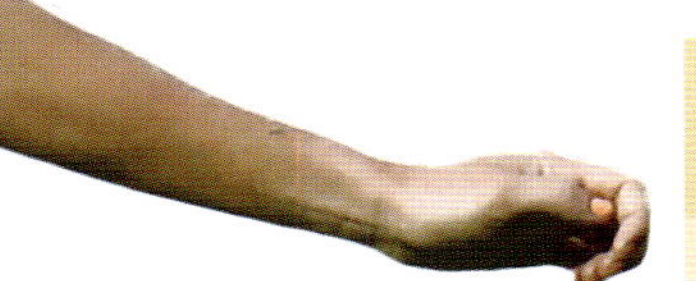

FACT BOX

First Season: 1985

Location: Charlottesville, Virginia

Stadium: Klöckner Stadium

Conference: Atlantic Coast Conference

All-Time Record: 580–205–85

NCAA Tournament Appearances: 36

College Cup Appearances: 3

National Titles: None

Top Coaches: Lauren Gregg (1986–95); April Heinrichs (1996–99); Steve Swanson (2000–)

Top Players: Amanda Cromwell (1988–91); Andrea Rubio (1989–92); Angela Hucles (1996–99); Becky Sauerbrunn (2003–07); Caroline Miller (2009–12); Morgan Brian (2011–14); Makenzy Doniak (2012–15); Lia Godfrey (2020–24)

Mascot: Cavman

WAKE FOREST DEMON DEACONS

Wake Forest players pose for a team photo before the 2024 College Cup semifinals.

Wake Forest started its women's soccer program in 1994. Many of its ACC rivals were already established. But the Demon Deacons started off strong. They reached the NCAA Tournament for the first time in 1996. That kicked off a run of 18 straight appearances.

One of Wake Forest's finest seasons came in 2010. Despite finishing fifth in the conference regular-season standings, the Demon Deacons got on a roll in the ACC Tournament.

After knocking off No. 9 Florida State 3–1, Wake Forest survived shootouts against No. 3 North Carolina and No. 4 Maryland to win its first conference tournament title.

A year later, the Demon Deacons went on their first deep NCAA Tournament run. In five games, star forward Katie Stengel had five goals and three assists.

SHOOTOUT THRILLER

Wake Forest and USC turned the 2024 Elite Eight into a thriller. The Demon Deacons took an early 1–0 lead, but USC responded with two second-half goals to go up 2–1. Wake Forest junior Alex Wood tied the game with ten minutes left. The teams then remained deadlocked through extra time. In the shootout, Demon Deacons goalkeeper Valentina Amaral stopped USC's first attempt. Wake Forest went on to win the shootout 4–3.

Tony da Luz took over as Wake Forest's coach in 1997 and remained in the role 28 seasons later.

Goalkeeper Aubrey Bledsoe posted three shutouts. However, Wake Forest's season ended after a 4–1 loss to ACC-rival Duke in the College Cup semifinals.

Despite continued success under longtime coach Tony da Luz, the Demon Deacons needed 13 years to get back to the College Cup. The 2024 team finished the season 16–4–4.

Wake Forest's Sierra Sythe dribbles past a Stanford defender in the 2024 College Cup semifinals.

Wake Forest beat Morehead State, Colorado, and Ohio State in the early rounds of the NCAA Tournament. The Demon Deacons then outlasted USC in a shootout to reach the College Cup. In the semifinals, senior midfielder Emily Morris scored with just over 17 minutes left to beat Stanford 1–0. But in the championship game, Wake Forest fell 1–0 to North Carolina.

FACT BOX

First Season: 1994

Location: Winston-Salem, North Carolina

Stadium: Spry Stadium

Conference: Atlantic Coast Conference

All-Time Record: 350–226–66

NCAA Tournament Appearances: 23

College Cup Appearances: 2

National Titles: None

Top Coaches: Tony da Luz (1997–)

Top Players: Anne Shropshire (1996–99); Emily Taggart (1998–2001); Joline Charlton (1999–2002); Sarah Kozey (2002–05); Jill Hutchinson (2006–09); Katie Stengel (2010–13); Aubrey Bledsoe (2010–13); Caiya Hanks (2022–24)

Mascot: The Demon Deacon

WISCONSIN BADGERS

The Wisconsin women's soccer program enjoyed a record-setting debut in 1981. In their first game, the Badgers poured in 18 goals against Beloit College, establishing a program record that still stood more than 40 years later. The win also set the tone for a strong decade in Madison.

Wisconsin's best stretch came in the late 1980s and early 1990s under future USWNT coach Greg Ryan. In 1988, the Badgers qualified for their second NCAA Tournament. They upset UConn in a shootout in an opening-round game played in snow. Then they knocked off Massachusetts 2–1 to reach their first College Cup. The run finally ended in the semifinals with a 3–0 loss to eventual champion North Carolina.

Wisconsin defender Camryn Biegalski controls the ball during a 2018 game against Memphis.

Wisconsin reached the College Cup again in 1991. Two of the program's legendary players guided the Badgers to victory over Colorado College in the semifinals. The program's all-time leading scorer, Kari Maijala, netted the only goal, while goalkeeper Heather Taggart kept the Tigers scoreless.

With the win, Wisconsin advanced to take on a North Carolina team seeking its ninth championship in ten seasons. The Tar Heels scored just 47 seconds into the game. They led 2–0 by the time Maijala scored Wisconsin's only goal on a penalty kick early in the second half. North Carolina won 3–1.

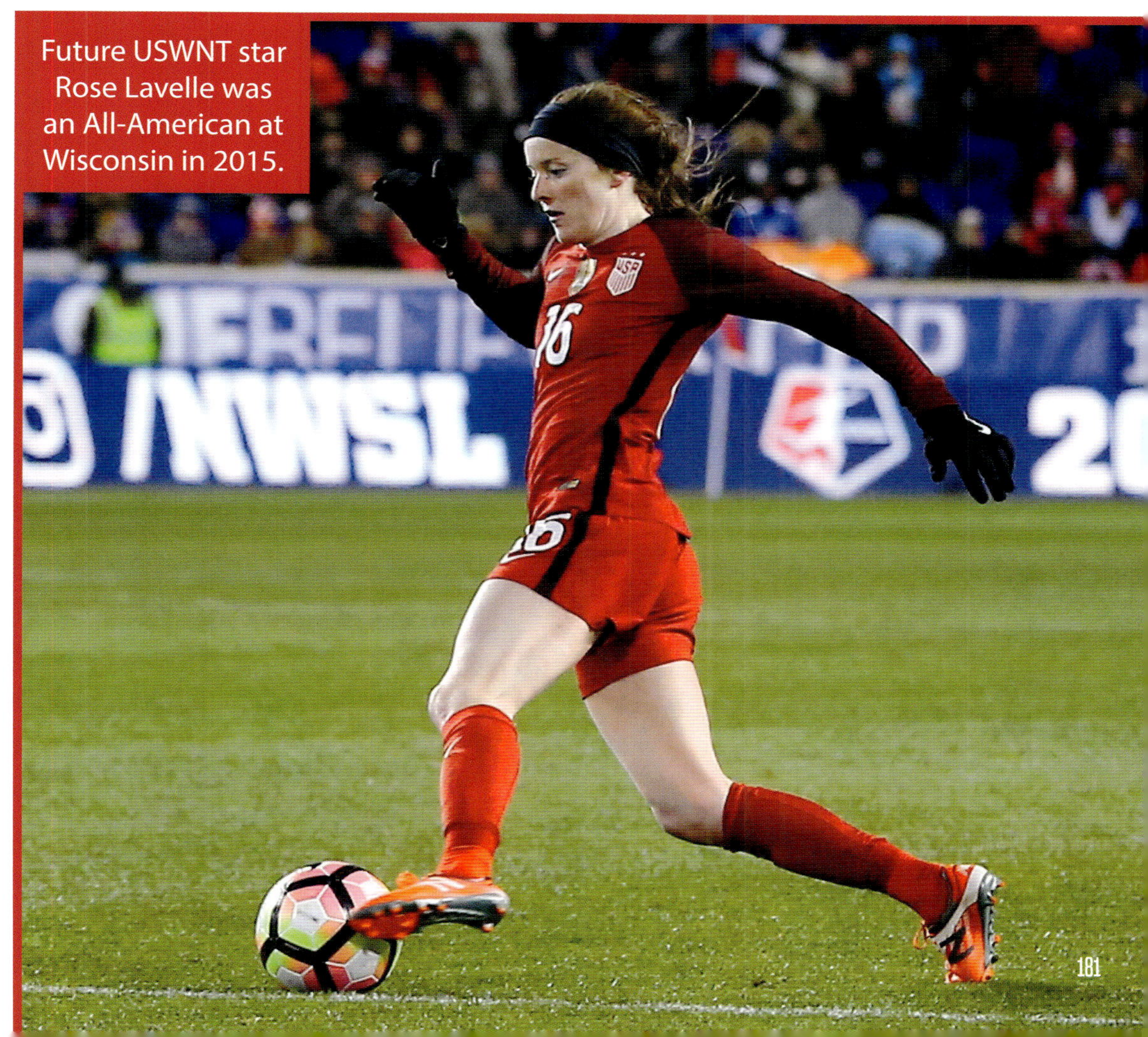

Future USWNT star Rose Lavelle was an All-American at Wisconsin in 2015.

In 2024, Wisconsin became the 13th team to reach the 500-victory mark. The Badgers reached the milestone with a 1–0 victory over rival Minnesota. Many of the victories have come under longtime coach Paula Wilkins. The veteran coach

Cara Walls, *right*, scored 42 goals in her Wisconsin career from 2011 to 2014.

took over a struggling team in 2007 and turned things around. Over the next 18 seasons, she coached the Badgers to a pair of Big Ten titles and 11 NCAA Tournament appearances.

SHUTOUT MASTER

Wisconsin goalkeeper Heather Taggart was the backbone of the team's successful stretch in the late 1980s and early 1990s. Taggart was known for her high-intensity, aggressive play. She compiled 52 shutouts in a career that ran from 1988 to 1991. Taggart held the record until UCLA's Katelyn Rowland broke it in 2014.

FACT BOX

First Season: 1981

Location: Madison, Wisconsin

Stadium: McClimon Soccer Complex

Conference: Big Ten Conference

All-Time Record: 505–259–101

NCAA Tournament Appearances: 24

College Cup Appearances: 2

National Titles: None

Top Coaches: Greg Ryan (1986–93); Paula Wilkins (2007–)

Top Players: Heather Taggart (1988–91); Kari Maijala (1988–91); Allison Wagner (1997–2000); Amy Vermeulen (2001–05); Cara Walls (2011–14); Rose Lavelle (2013–16); Dani Rhodes (2016–19); Emma Jaskaniec (2019–23)

Mascot: Bucky Badger

ALL-TIME NCAA RECORDS

MEN'S RECORDS

Career Goals
Thompson Usiyan, Appalachian State (1977–80): 109

Career Assists
Dante Washington, Radford (1988–92): 66

Career Points
Thompson Usiyan, Appalachian State (1977–80): 255

Career Saves
Jose Grave de Peralta, Wake Forest (1980–83): 620

Career Shutouts
David Meves, Akron (2009–12): 55

Single-Season Goals
Thompson Usiyan, Appalachian State (1980): 46

Single-Season Assists
Ben Ferry, George Washington (1997): 24

Single-Season Points
Thompson Usiyan, Appalachian State (1980): 108

Single-Season Saves
Ray Migas, DePaul (1987): 230

Single-Season Shutouts
John Putna, Indiana (1979): 18
David Meves, Akron (2009): 18
Trey Muse, Indiana (2017): 18

LOUISVILLE
24
F50

WOMEN'S RECORDS

Career Goals
Danielle Fotopoulos, SMU/Florida (1994–96, 1998): 118

Career Assists
Holly Manthei, Notre Dame (1994–97): 129

Career Points
Danielle Fotopoulos, SMU/Florida (1994–96, 1998): 284

Career Saves
Beth Zack, Marist (1995–98): 704

Career Shutouts
Katelyn Rowland, UCLA (2011–14): 55

Single-Season Goals
Christine Sinclair, Portland (2005): 39

Single-Season Assists
Holly Manthei, Notre Dame (1996): 44

Single-Season Points
Mia Hamm, North Carolina (1992): 97

Single-Season Saves
Dayna DiCesare, Robert Morris (1993): 343

Single-Season Shutouts
Cassie Miller, Florida State (2014): 19
Katelyn Rowland, UCLA (2014): 19
Casey Murphy, Rutgers (2015): 19

ORTLAND
3

GLOSSARY

All-America
Designation for players chosen as the best amateurs in the country in a particular sport.

assist
A pass, shot, or deflection that leads directly to a teammate's goal.

captain
The team leader and the only player allowed to speak to game officials regarding the rules.

dynasty
An extended period of excellence or success for a team.

extra time
Time added to a soccer tournament game if the score is tied after regulation.

favorite
The person or team that is expected to win.

free kick
An unguarded kick awarded to a team after an opponent's foul.

pandemic
A widespread outbreak of a disease that affects a large portion of the population.

penalty kick
A play in which a shooter faces a goalkeeper alone.

point
A statistic used in college soccer. Goals are worth two points and assists count as one point.

retire
To end one's career.

rival
An opponent with whom a player or team has a fierce and ongoing competition.

scholarship
Money provided to a student to pay for his or her education.

seed
A rank assigned to a player or team in a tournament.

shootout
In soccer, a series of penalty kicks held after extra time to decide who wins a game.

underdog
The person or team that is not expected to win.

upset
To unexpectedly beat a team that was heavily favored to win.

volley
To kick a ball out of the air rather than off the ground.

TO LEARN MORE

FURTHER READINGS

Clarke, David J. *Everything Soccer*. Abdo, 2024.

Ellis, Abigail, ed. *Illustrated Sports Encyclopedia*. DK Penguin Random House, 2023.

Flynn, Brendan. *World Soccer Encyclopedia*. Abdo, 2025.

ONLINE RESOURCES

To learn more about college soccer, please visit **abdobooklinks.com** or scan this QR code. These links are routinely monitored and updated to provide the most current information available.

INDEX

PHOTO CREDITS

Cover Photos: Andy Mead/YCJ/Corbis/Icon Sportswire/Getty Images, front (Catrina Atanda); Ben McKeown/AP Images, front (Daryl Dike); Andy Mead/ISI Photos/Getty Images, front (Zach Barrett, Adrian Schulze Solano); Rodolfo Gonzalez/NCAA Photos/Getty Images, front (Christine Sinclair, Megan Rapinoe); Jamie Schwaberow/NCAA Photos/Getty Images, front (Ousmane Sylla); Grant Halverson/NCAA Photos/Getty Images, front (Chris Gbandi); Lincoln University/Historically Black Colleges & Universities/Getty Images, back (Lincoln team); Isaiah Vazquez/NCAA Photos via Getty Images/Getty Images, back (trophy)
Interior Photos: Jamie Schwaberow/NCAA Photos/Getty Images, 1, 2–3, 4–5, 14–15, 21, 22, 25, 26, 48, 49, 50, 53, 54–55, 61, 78, 95, 99, 102, 105, 114–115, 132, 141, 153, 154, 170, 184–185; Lincoln University/Historically Black Colleges & Universities/Getty Images, 7; Paul A. Souders/Corbis Historical/Getty Images, 9; Brian Westerholt/Four Seam Images/AP Images, 10; Stephen Dunn/Allsport/Getty Images Sport/Getty Images, 12; Rick Stewart/Allsport/Getty Images Sport/Getty Images, 13; Dave Martin/AP Images, 16, 46; Ben McKeown/AP Images, 17, 128, 142; Andy Mead/YCJ/Icon Sportswire/Getty Images, 18–19, 38, 62, 100, 111, 119; Brian A. Westerholt/Getty Images Sport/Getty Images, 20; Jon Ferrey/Allsport/Getty Images Sport/Getty Images, 24; Bob Child/AP Images, 28; David Roberts/Hartford Courant/AP Images, 29; Grant Halverson/NCAA Photos/Getty Images, 30–31, 82, 88, 89, 112, 134–135, 165, 176, 177, 178–179; Nati Harnik/AP Images, 32; Creighton Athletics, 33; Charles Brock/Icon Sportswire/AP Images, 34; Andy Mead/Corbis/Icon Sportswire/Getty Images, 36; Andy Mead/YCJ/Icon SMI/Corbis/Icon Sportswire/Getty Images, 37; Chuck Myers/MCT/Tribune News Service/Getty Images, 40; Gregg Forwerck/NCAA Photos/Getty Images, 41; Tony Quinn/Icon Sportswire/Getty Images, 42, 52; Jamie Sabau/NCAA Photos/Getty Images, 44; Tony Quinn/Getty Images Sport/Getty Images, 45; MSU Athletic Communications, 56–57; Tony Quinn/Icon Sportswire/AP Images, 57; Joshua Blanchard/Getty Images for TAG Heuer/Getty Images Entertainment/Getty Images, 58; Chris Putnam/AP Images, 60; T. Quinn/WireImage/Getty Images Sport/Getty Images, 64; Ben Solomon/NCAA Photos/Getty Images, 66; Michelle Hutchins/NCAA Photos/Getty Images, 67; Andy Mead/ISI Photos/Getty Images, 68, 70–71, 81, 90, 92–93; Eakin Howard/Getty Images Sport/Getty Images, 69, 166–167; Rick Ulreich/Icon Sportswire/AP Images, 72; Jamie Squire/Allsport/Getty Images Sport/Getty Images, 73; Rick Ulreich/Icon Sportswire/Getty Images, 74; Paul Buck/NCAA Photos/Getty Images, 76; Justin Tafoya/NCAA Photos/Getty Images, 77; Andy Mead/YCJ/Corbis/Icon Sportswire/Getty Images, 80, 96, 110, 118; Doug Pensinger/Allsport/Getty Images Sport/Getty Images, 84; Daniel P. Derella/AP Images, 85; Bud Symes/Allsport/Getty Images Sport/Getty Images, 86; Isaiah Vazquez/Getty Images Sport/Getty Images, 92; Bernd Weissbrod/picture alliance/dpa/AP Images, 94; T. Quinn/WireImage/Getty Images, 98; Erin Chang/ISI Photos/Getty Images, 103, 127; Thien-An Truong/ISI Photos/Getty Images, 106; Paul Chinn/San Francisco Chronicle/Hearst Newspapers/Getty Images, 107; Andy Mead/YCJ/Icon Sportswire/AP Images, 108, 172; Kirby Lee/Getty Images Sport/Getty Images, 115; Chuck Myers/Cal Sport Media/Zuma Wire/AP Images, 116; Chris Leduc/Icon Sportswire/Getty Images, 120; Andy Mead/YCJ/Icon Sportswire, 122, 124; Alan Campbell, 123; Trevor Brown Jr./NCAA Photos/Getty Images, 126, 168, 169; David Madison/Getty Images Sport/Getty Images, 130; Will & Deni McIntyre/The Chronicle Collection/Getty Images, 131; John Joyner/NCAA Photos/Getty Images, 134; Sara D. Davis/AP Images, 136–137; Jim R. Bounds/AP Images, 137; Jeffrey Camarati/NCAA Photos/Getty Images, 138; Pat Little/AP Images, 140; Darren Abate/Getty Images Sport/Getty Images, 144, 145, 146–147, 164, 187; Stephen Dunn/Getty Images Sport/Getty Images, 148–149; Rich Graessle/Icon Sportswire/Getty Images, 149, 150, 181; Alison Woodworth/NCAA Photos/Getty Images, 152; Matthew Huang/Icon Sportswire/AP Images, 156; Jeffrey Camarati/NCAA Photos/Getty Images, 157; Cody Glenn/Getty Images Sport/Getty Images, 158; Jaye Howell/WireImage/Getty Images Sport/Getty Images, 160; Stuart Villanueva/College Station Eagle/AP Images, 161; Sam Craft/The Bryan-College Station Eagle/AP Images, 162; Ira Black/Corbis Sport/Getty Images, 173; Andrew Shurtleff/The Daily Progress/AP Images, 174–175; Kevin Langley/Cal Sport Media/Alamy Live News/Alamy, 180; John Mersits/Sout/Zuma Press, Inc./Alamy, 182

ABDOBOOKS.COM

Published by Abdo Reference, a division of ABDO, PO Box 398166, Minneapolis, Minnesota 55439.

Printed in China.
102025
012026

Editor: Chrös McDougall
Series Designer: Colleen McLaren
Production Designer: Karli Hughes

LIBRARY OF CONGRESS CONTROL NUMBER: 2025939302

PUBLISHER'S CATALOGING-IN-PUBLICATION DATA

Names: Beattie, Charlie, author.
Title: The college soccer encyclopedia / by Charlie Beattie
Description: Minneapolis, Minnesota: Abdo Reference, 2026 | Series: College sports encyclopedias | Includes online resources and index.
Identifiers: ISBN 9781098298845 (lib. bdg.) | ISBN 9798384932642 (ebook)
Subjects: LCSH: Soccer--Juvenile literature. | European football--Juvenile literature. | College sports--Juvenile literature. | Soccer teams--Juvenile literature. | Soccer--Records--Juvenile literature. | Sports--United States--History--Juvenile literature. | Encyclopedias--Juvenile literature.
Classification: DDC 796.334--dc23